Standards and policy statements
of special interest to women workers

Selected standards and policy statements of special interest to women workers adopted under the auspices of the International Labour Office

International Labour Office   Geneva

Copyright © International Labour Organisation 1980

Publications of the International Labour Office enjoy copyright under Protocol 2 of the Universal Copyright Convention. Nevertheless, short excerpts from them may be reproduced without authorisation, on condition that the source is indicated. For rights of reproduction or translation, application should be made to the Editorial and Translation Branch, International Labour Office, CH-1211 Geneva 22, Switzerland. The International Labour Office welcomes such applications.

ISBN 92-2-102441-5 (limp cover)
ISBN 92-2-102418-0 (hard cover)

First published 1980

The designations employed in ILO publications, which are in conformity with United Nations practice, and the presentation of material therein do not imply the expression of any opinion whatsoever on the part of the International Labour Office concerning the legal status of any country or territory or of its authorities, or concerning the delimitation of its frontiers.
The responsibility for opinions expressed in signed articles, studies and other contributions rests solely with their authors, and publication does not constitute an endorsement by the International Labour Office of the opinions expressed in them.

ILO publications can be obtained through major booksellers or ILO local offices in many countries, or direct from ILO Publications, International Labour Office, CH-1211 Geneva 22, Switzerland. A catalogue or list of new publications will be sent free of charge from the above address.

Printed in Switzerland

CONTENTS

Introduction 1

1. **Basic human rights** 5
   Elimination of Discrimination against Women and Promotion of Equality of Opportunity and Treatment for them in Employment and Related Matters. Texts of General Scope 5
   Equal Remuneration for Men and Women 41

2. **Employment policy and human resources development** 49
   Employment Policy 49
   Human Resources Development 54

3. **Conditions of work and social policy** 63
   Night Work 63
   Hours of Work 65
   Occupational Safety, Health and Welfare 68
   Facilities and Services for Women Workers with Family Responsibilities 75

4. **Social security** 83
   Maternity Protection 83
   Survivors' Benefit 97

5. **Industrial relations** 107

6. **Selected categories of workers** 111
   Domestic Workers 111
   Home Workers 112
   Migrant Workers 114
   Nursing Personnel 118
   Plantations 121
   Teachers 128

7. **Labour administration** 131

INTRODUCTION

The purpose of this compilation is to present in a single document selected provisions of international instruments and policy statements of special concern to women which have been adopted under the auspices of the International Labour Organisation.

Since the creation of the International Labour Organisation in 1919, the principle of equal treatment for women workers, including equal pay, has been embodied in its Constitution. This principle has been reaffirmed by the Declaration of Philadelphia (1944), annexed to the Constitution, which proclaims that: all human beings, irrespective of race, creed or sex, have the right to pursue their material well-being and spiritual development in conditions of freedom and dignity, economic security and equal opportunity.

The International Labour Organisation has always given continuing attention to the problems of women workers. The various aspects of these problems have been examined at the International Labour Conference, the regional ILO conferences and at meetings of Industrial Committees and other specialised bodies of the ILO. It is appropriate to recall the functions of these meetings and the particular nature of texts adopted by them.

The principal task of the International Labour Conference which meets once a year and in the deliberations of which workers' and employers' representatives participate on an equal footing with governments is to discuss and adopt international instruments laying down minimum labour standards. These instruments take the form of either an international labour Convention or Recommendation; Conventions and Recommendations are adopted by the Conference by a two-thirds majority. The Conference also reviews each year the general world situation with regard to social and economic matters, and, within this context, adopts resolutions bearing on economic and social policy.

Conventions[1] are communicated to the governments of member States of the ILO, who have to submit them to the competent national authorities. Each State remains free to decide whether it wishes to ratify a Convention or not, but when it does ratify any Convention, the State concerned is legally

Standards and policy statements of special interest to women workers

bound to take such measures as would be necessary to give full effect to all the provisions of the said Convention and to report to the ILO on these measures.[2]

Recommendations are standard-defining instruments and are not subject to ratification; they are to be communicated to all Members for consideration with a view to effect being given to them by national legislation or otherwise.

Resolutions adopted by the Conference relate to questions of economic and social policy; some of these resolutions deal wholly or in part with women workers' problems.

Regional ILO conferences examine questions which are of particular interest to the region concerned, and their conclusions take the form of resolutions or reports addressed to the Governing Body which transmits them to the governments concerned; they are not binding on the latter in any manner. However, experience shows that these texts exercise a real influence on the evolution of social policy in the various regions.

Industrial Committees and similar meetings examine the special problems of some of the major industries and specific branches of economic activity; they are tripartite in composition and their conclusions or resolutions relate to problems arising in specific branches of activity; they serve as a guide to national social policies and seek to promote, in the different countries, a policy of social progress in the industries or branches of economic activity concerned.

The material presented in this document is extracted from texts adopted by these various meetings.

The compilation is set out under various subject headings. In addition to a section containing texts of general scope regarding elimination of discrimination against women and promotion of equality of opportunity and treatment for them in employment and related matters, the compilation comprises sections dealing with equal remuneration for men and women; employment policy and human resources development; conditions of work and social policy; social security, including maternity protection; industrial relations; selected categories of workers, and labour administration.

The compilation is intended to provide an indication of the standards and principles which have been laid down on the subject with which it is concerned, and not to be an exhaustive collection of all instruments ever adopted or statements made by ILO bodies and meetings on a given topic. Accordingly, where the same standard or principle is to be found in several texts, only the most authoritative, comprehensive or up-to-date text is included.[3]

It is hoped that this document will be used as a guide to national social and labour policies for those who deal with equality of opportunity and treatment for women workers, especially government officials, leaders of organisations of employers and workers and women's organisations.

The publication of this document was financed by a grant of the Voluntary Fund for the United Nations Decade for Women.

Introduction

Notes

[1] Nearly all the Conventions and Recommendations apply to both men and women workers and cover a wide range of subjects and all categories of workers. Among these instruments a number are of special concern to women workers. Relatively few Conventions and Recommendations apply solely to women. Those that do are of two main types–protective and promotional. The former are concerned with providing women workers with the special protection they were considered to require because of both physiological and social factors. The latter are designed to secure for women the same rights and treatment as those enjoyed by men.

[2] At the time of preparing the present compilation, the total number of ratifications was over 4,800. Promotion of the ratification and supervision of the implementation of Conventions represents an important and continuing aspect of ILO regular activities.

[3] The Governing Body of the ILO at its 209th (February-March 1979) Session approved a classification of existing instruments (Conventions and Recommendations) into three categories (1: existing instruments, ratification and application of which should be promoted on a priority basis; 2: existing instruments, revision of which would be appropriate; 3: other existing instruments) and a list of possible subjects for new standards for inclusion in a fourth category. A number of instruments have been included in both categories 1 and 2. This indicates that, while they constitute the most recent ILO standards on the subject and remain a valid target, there are certain respects in which their revision would be appropriate. Instruments classified in category 3 have not been included in the compilation except in one instance.

BASIC HUMAN RIGHTS   1

ELIMINATION OF DISCRIMINATION AGAINST WOMEN
AND PROMOTION OF EQUALITY OF OPPORTUNITY AND TREATMENT
FOR THEM IN EMPLOYMENT AND CONNECTED MATTERS.
TEXTS OF GENERAL SCOPE

Texts adopted by the International Labour Conference

(1) Discrimination (Employment and Occupation) Convention, 1958 (No. 111)

. . . .

Article 1 [1]

1. For the purpose of this Convention the term "discrimination" includes—

(a) any distinction, exclusion or preference made on the basis of race, colour, sex, religion, political opinion, national extraction or social origin, which has the effect of nullifying or impairing equality of opportunity or treatment in employment or occupation;

(b) such other distinction, exclusion or preference which has the effect of nullifying or impairing equality of opportunity or treatment in employment or occupation as may be determined by the Member concerned after consultation with representative employers' and workers' organisations, where such exist, and with other appropriate bodies.

2. Any distinction, exclusion or preference in respect of a particular job based on the inherent requirements thereof shall not be deemed to be discrimination.

3. For the purpose of this Convention the terms "employment" and "occupation" include access to vocational training, access to employment and to particular occupations, and terms and conditions of employment.

Article 2

Each Member for which this Convention is in force undertakes to declare and pursue a national policy designed to promote, by methods appropriate to national conditions and practice, equality of opportunity and treatment in respect of employment and occupation, with a view to eliminating any discrimination in respect thereof.

Article 3

Each Member for which this Convention is in force undertakes, by methods appropriate to national conditions and practice–

(a) to seek the co-operation of employers' and workers' organisations and other appropriate bodies in promoting the acceptance and observance of this policy;

(b) to enact such legislation and to promote such educational programmes as may be calculated to secure the acceptance and observance of the policy;

(c) to repeal any statutory provisions and modify any administrative instructions or practices which are inconsistent with the policy;

(d) to pursue the policy in respect of employment under the direct control of a national authority;

(e) to ensure observance of the policy in the activities of vocational guidance, vocational training and placement services under the direction of a national authority;

(f) to indicate in its annual reports on the application of the Convention the action taken in pursuance of the policy and the results secured by such action.

. . . .

Article 5

1. Special measures of protection or assistance provided for in other Conventions or Recommendations adopted by the International Labour Conference shall not be deemed to be discrimination.

2. Any Member may, after consultation with representative employers' and workers' organisations, where such exist, determine that other special measures designed to meet the particular requirements of persons who, for reasons such as sex, age, disablement, family responsibilities or social or cultural status, are generally recognised to require special protection or assistance, shall not be deemed to be discrimination.

Article 6

Each Member which ratifies this Convention undertakes to apply it to non-metropolitan territories in accordance with the provisions of the Constitution of the International Labour Organisation.

. . . .

(1) Discrimination (Employment and Occupation) Recommendation, 1958 (No. 111)

II. FORMULATION AND APPLICATION OF POLICY

2. Each Member should formulate a national policy for the prevention of discrimination in employment and occupation. This policy should be applied by means of legislative measures, collective agreements between representative employers' and workers' organisations or in any other manner consistent with national conditions and practice, and should have regard to the following principles:

(a) the promotion of equality of opportunity and treatment in employment and occupation is a matter of public concern;

(b) all persons should, without discrimination, enjoy equality of opportunity and treatment in respect of–
   (i) access to vocational guidance and placement services;
   (ii) access to training and employment of their own choice on the basis of individual suitability for such training or employment;
   (iii) advancement in accordance with their individual character, experience, ability and diligence;
   (iv) security of tenure of employment;
   (v) remuneration for work of equal value;
   (vi) conditions of work including hours of work, rest periods, annual holidays with pay, occupational safety and occupational health measures, as well as social security measures and welfare facilities and benefits provided in connection with employment;

(c) government agencies should apply non-discriminatory employment policies in all their activities;

(d) employers should not practise or countenance discrimination in engaging or training any person for employment, in advancing or retaining such person in employment, or in fixing terms and conditions of employment; nor should any person or organisation obstruct or interfere, either directly or indirectly, with employers in pursuing this principle;

(e) in collective negotiations and industrial relations the parties should respect the principle of equality of opportunity and treatment in employment and occupation and should ensure that collective agreements contain no provisions of a discriminatory character in respect of access to, training for, advancement in or retention of employment or in respect of the terms and conditions of employment;

(f) employers' and workers' organisations should not practise or countenance discrimination in respect of admission, retention of membership or participation in their affairs.

Standards and policy statements of special interest to women workers

3. Each Member should–
(a) ensure application of the principles of non-discrimination–
- (i) in respect of employment under the direct control of a national authority;
- (ii) in the activities of vocational guidance, vocational training and placement services under the direction of a national authority;

(b) promote their observance, where practicable and necessary, in respect of other employment and other vocational guidance, vocational training and placement services by such methods as–
- (i) encouraging state, provincial or local government departments or agencies and industries and undertakings operated under public ownership or control to ensure the application of the principles;
- (ii) making eligibility for contracts involving the expenditure of public funds dependent on observance of the principles;
- (iii) making eligibility for grants to training establishments and for a licence to operate a private employment agency or a private vocational guidance office dependent on observance of the principles.

4. Appropriate agencies, to be assisted where practicable by advisory committees composed of representatives of employers' and workers' organisations, where such exist, and of other interested bodies, should be established for the purpose of promoting application of the policy in all fields of public and private employment, and in particular–

(a) to take all practicable measures to foster public understanding and acceptance of the principles of non-discrimination;

(b) to receive, examine and investigate complaints that the policy it not being observed and, if necessary by conciliation, to secure the correction of any practices regarded as in conflict with the policy; and

(c) to consider further any complaints which cannot be effectively settled by conciliation and to render opinions or issue decisions concerning the manner in which discriminatory practices revealed should be corrected.

5. Each Member should repeal any statutory provisions and modify any administrative instructions or practices which are inconsistent with the policy.

6. Application of the policy should not adversely affect special measures designed to meet the particular requirements of persons who, for reasons such as sex, age, disablement, family responsibilities or social or cultural status are generally recognised to require special protection or assistance.

. . . .

9. There should be continuing co-operation between the competent authorities, representatives of employers and workers and appropriate bodies to consider what further positive measures may be necessary in the light of national conditions to put the principles of non-discrimination into effect.

III. Co-ordination of Measures for the Prevention of Discrimination in All Fields

10. The authorities responsible for action against discrimination in employment and occupation should co-operate closely and continuously with the authorities responsible for action against discrimination in other fields in order that measures taken in all fields may be co-ordinated.

(1) Social Policy (Basic Aims and Standards) Convention, 1962 (No. 117)

. . . .

Part V. Non-Discrimination on Grounds of Race, Colour, Sex, Belief, Tribal Association or Trade Union Affiliation

Article 14

1. It shall be an aim of policy to abolish all discrimination among workers on grounds of race, colour, sex, belief, tribal association or trade union affiliation in respect of—

(a) labour legislation and agreements which shall afford equitable economic treatment to all those lawfully resident or working in the country;
(b) admission to public or private employment;
(c) conditions of engagement and promotion;
(d) opportunities for vocational training;
(e) conditions of work;
(f) health, safety and welfare measures;
(g) discipline;
(h) participation in the negotiation of collective agreements;
(i) wage rates, which shall be fixed according to the principle of equal pay for work of equal value in the same operation and undertaking.

2. All practicable measures shall be taken to lessen, by raising the rates applicable to the lower-paid workers, any existing differences in wage rates due to discrimination by reason of race, colour, sex, belief, tribal association or trade union affiliation.

3. Workers from one country engaged for employment in another country may be granted in addition to their wages benefits in cash or in kind to meet any reasonable personal or family expenses resulting from employment away from their homes.

4. The foregoing provisions of this Article shall be without prejudice to such measures as the competent authority may think it necessary or desirable

Standards and policy statements of special interest to women workers

to take for the safeguarding of motherhood and for ensuring the health, safety and welfare of women workers.

PART VI. EDUCATION AND TRAINING

Article 15

1. Adequate provision shall be made to the maximum extent possible under local conditions, for the progressive development of broad systems of education, vocational training and apprenticeship, with a view to the effective preparation of children and young persons of both sexes for a useful occupation.

. . . .

(1 and 2)   Termination of Employment Recommendation, 1963 (No. 119)

. . . .

2. (1) Termination of employment should not take place unless there is a valid reason for such termination connected with the capacity or conduct of the worker or based on the operational requirements of the undertaking, establishment or service.

. . . .

3. The following, inter alia, should not constitute valid reasons for termination of employment:

. . . .

(c) the filing in good faith of a complaint or the participation in a proceeding against an employer involving alleged violation of laws or regulations; or
(d) race, colour, sex, marital status, religion, political opinion, national extraction or social origin.

4. A worker who feels that his employment has been unjustifiably terminated should be entitled, unless the matter has been satisfactorily determined through such procedures within the undertaking, establishment or service, as may exist or be established consistent with this Recommendation, to appeal, within a reasonable time, against that termination with the assistance, where the worker so requests, of a person representing him to a body established under a collective agreement or to a neutral body such as a court, an arbitrator, an arbitration committee or a similar body.

5. (1) The bodies referred to in Paragraph 4 should be empowered to examine the reasons given for the termination of employment and the other circumstances relating to the case and to render a decision on the justification of the termination.

. . . .

6. The bodies referred to in Paragraph 4 should be empowered, if they find that the termination of employment was unjustified, to order that the worker concerned, unless reinstated, where appropriate with payment of unpaid wages, should be paid adequate compensation, or afforded such other relief as may be determined under the methods of implementation set out in Paragraph 1, or granted such compensation and other relief as may be so determined.

. . . .

Resolution concerning Women Workers in a Changing World, adopted by the International Labour Conference at its 48th Session (Geneva, 1964)

The General Conference of the International Labour Organisation,

Conscious of the increasingly important role played by women in modern society and of the fact that their work is necessary to the development of the productive forces of their countries,

Noting that the number of women who work outside their homes has increased considerably in numerous countries and that this tendency, although particularly marked in the industrial countries, is also noticeable in the economically developing countries,

Considering that in principle the problems of women workers should not be distinguished from those of men workers and that they should be solved within the same general framework of policy and action but that it is nevertheless certain that women have to face special problems deriving both from various discriminations and from their multiple responsibilities,

Noting that even in the countries which are economically and socially very advanced, despite the great progress which has been made, women workers still are often subject to discrimination,

Noting, furthermore, that in some developing countries the problems which women workers have to face are to a great extent the reflection of low levels of economic growth and are aggravated by illiteracy, which is more widespread amongst women than men, by lack of education, lack of vocational training and lack of employment,

Considering that it is necessary to adapt attitudes and social legislation relating to the employment of women to new tendencies and to recognise the right to work for women and the value of their contribution to economic activity by encouraging all action aimed at eliminating any discrimination against them,

Considering that the International Labour Organisation has established standards directed towards the attainment of these ends and that many member States have not yet formally accepted the instruments in question;

Standards and policy statements of special interest to women workers

1. Urgently appeals to member States to take all possible steps—

(a) to ratify and implement fully the Equal Remuneration Convention, 1951, and the Discrimination (Employment and Occupation) Convention, 1958; and

(b) to implement in respect of girls and women the provisions of the Vocational Training Recommendation, 1962;

2. Requests all States Members of the International Labour Organisation to consider the desirability of taking appropriate steps—

(a) to establish within the framework of national administration or any other appropriate organisation a central unit for co-ordinating research, planning, programming and action on women workers' opportunities, needs and problems;

(b) to develop systematic arrangements for consulting employers' and workers' organisations and other organisations primarily concerned; and

(c) to encourage the dissemination of information regarding all aspects of women's employment and conditions of work;

. . . .

Resolution concerning the Economic and Social Advancement of Women in Developing Countries, adopted by the International Labour Conference at its 48th Session (Geneva, 1964)

The General Conference of the International Labour Organisation,

Recognising the urgency of taking all possible steps to raise the economic and social status of women and of integrating them more closely and effectively into the whole process of developing human resources which is characteristic of our era,

Recognising that the present status of women in developing countries and the problems of women workers in such countries are, to a great extent, the reflection of the very low levels of their economic growth,

Recognising that the needs and problems of women workers in the developing countries are particularly urgent,

Taking into account the fact that these problems, arising within a different context of political, economic, social and cultural development in each of the developing countries, will influence such measures as may be taken to advance the status of women;

1. Requests developing countries, which are member States of the International Labour Organisation, to give special priority in their national plans to assisting women to integrate themselves into the national economic life and improve their status with particular reference to the following problems:

Basic human rights

(a) the need for providing increased and better educational facilities for girls and women, including facilities for vocational, technical and professional training at all levels;
(b) the need to widen the framework of employment opportunities for girls and women, particularly in the non-agricultural sector of the economy;
(c) the need to develop suitable forms of vocational guidance and employment counselling and assistance;
(d) the need to formulate and implement non-discriminatory practices and policies in this field, and to mobilise public opinion to this end;
(e) the need to include women in all social security measures according to their real needs and without prejudice to their employment opportunities;
(f) the need to make efforts to raise the status of women, particularly in rural areas;
(g) the need to develop means to improve the conditions of women working in agriculture, cottage industries and marketing, and of supervising and improving conditions of work in these sectors; and
(h) the need for promotional efforts to change the economic and social climate within which women seek and find employment in order to enable them to respond to the changing needs of national development and to contribute as effectively as possible to the varying demands placed on them, taking into consideration that family responsibilities should not be a handicap for women to play their full part in economic and social life;

2. Calls upon the International Labour Organisation to expand and intensify its programme of activity directed expressly towards the economic and social advancement of women workers in developing countries;

3. Requests the International Labour Organisation to organise as soon as possible regional meetings on women workers in a changing world.

Declaration on Equality of Opportunity and Treatment for Women Workers adopted by the International Labour Conference at its 60th Session (Geneva, 1975)

The General Conference of the International Labour Organisation,

On the basis of the Universal Declaration of Human Rights, reaffirming the principle of non-discrimination and proclaiming that all human beings are born free and equal in dignity and before the law, and declaring that all efforts must be made to provide every worker, without distinction on grounds of sex, with equality of opportunity and treatment in all social, cultural, economic, civic and political fields,

Conscious of the resolutions, declarations, covenants, Conventions and Recommendations of the United Nations and the specialised agencies, particularly the instruments adopted by the International Labour Organisation designed to eliminate discrimination against women and to promote equality of opportunity and treatment for them,

Convinced of the special importance of the guarantee of equal rights and opportunities for men and women in their economic and social life and in social development,

Aware of the great economic, social and cultural differences existing among the various regions and countries of the world and among areas within countries and which condition the rate of progress towards greater equality of opportunity and treatment,

Considering that the establishment of a new international economic and social order in accordance with United Nations Resolutions will contribute towards ensuring better employment, conditions of work and life for women, especially in developing countries,

Aware of the need to devote particular attention to the situation of women in countries under foreign domination or subject to the practices of apartheid,

Aware of the invaluable role of women workers in every national economy and of the need to enable women to exercise their right to gainful employment, regardless of family situation, on a footing of equality with men and to maximise their contribution to development,

Aware that the position of women cannot be changed without changing also the role of men in society and in the family,

Concerned that considerable discrimination against women workers persists and is incompatible with the interests of the economy, the development of social progress, social justice, the fundamental rights of men and women, and the welfare of the family and society,

Convinced that women's lack of vocational qualifications is one of the causes of such discrimination,

Convinced that all efforts must be made to promote and ensure equality of opportunity and treatment for women workers in law and practice,

Conscious of the important responsibility and contribution of the ILO in stimulating efforts to this end,

Aware also of the needs of developing countries and the need to achieve full employment as a basis for more balanced and equitable economic and social development,

Conscious that women's problems in the world of work can be approached and solved only within the same general framework of economic and social development as those of men,

Believing that a long-term programme of practical international action will improve the situation of women and increase their effective participation in all sectors,

Basic human rights

Desirous therefore of setting forth certain principles as targets to be achieved progressively in relation to the integration of women in economic life, understanding that such integration presupposes deliberate planning of different social functions;

Solemnly proclaims this Declaration on the occasion of International Women's Year:

Article 1

(1) There shall be equality of opportunity and treatment for all workers. All forms of discrimination on grounds of sex which deny or restrict such equality are unacceptable and must be eliminated.

(2) Positive special treatment during a transitional period aimed at effective equality between the sexes shall not be regarded as discriminatory.

Article 2

In the promotion of equality of opportunity and treatment between women and men in economic and social life, full account shall be taken of the principles contained in international resolutions, declarations, covenants, Conventions and Recommendations adopted by the United Nations and by the specialised agencies relating to the prevention of discrimination against women.

Article 3

All measures shall be taken to guarantee women's right to work as the inalienable right of every human being and to revise, as necessary, existing laws, collective agreements, practices or customs which limit the integration of women in the workforce on a footing of equality with men.

Article 4

All measures shall be taken to educate public opinion and to foster social attitudes and behaviour which encourage and ensure equality between women and men in working, family and social life.

Article 5

(1) Measures shall be taken to ensure that boys and girls receive the same basic education and have access to the same forms of vocational orientation and guidance and to all forms and levels of basic vocational training for all occupations and professions in accordance with the principles laid down in the Recommendation concerning human resources development adopted by the Conference at its 60th Session.

(2) Measures shall be taken to urge institutes of vocational guidance and training to help and to encourage girls and women to make full use of available orientation guidance and training facilities and to choose and enter all occupations freely, including those hitherto reserved in practice for men.

(3) Measures shall be taken to ensure the placement of girls and women who have completed training programmes on an equal footing with similarly qualified boys and men. For this purpose, maximum encouragement should be given to co-operation between training instructors and the official placement services.

(4) Measures shall be taken to prohibit stipulations regarding the sex of applicants in public employment notices.

(5) Special measures shall be taken to facilitate the continuing education and training of women on the same basis as men and to provide retraining facilities for them, especially during and after periods of absence from the labour force.

Article 6

(1) With a view to stimulating women's integration in the workforce on a footing of equality with men, all measures shall be taken to encourage a more equitable balance in their distribution in the various sectors of the economy, in the various branches, professions and occupations and the various levels of skill and responsibility.

(2) In accordance with the provisions of the Discrimination (Employment and Occupation) Convention, 1958 (No. 111), and of the Discrimination (Employment and Occupation) Recommendation, 1958 (No. 111), there shall be no discrimination on the grounds of sex in employment or occupation.

(3) There shall be no discrimination against women workers on the grounds of marital status, age or family responsibilities.

(4) Special measures shall be taken to ensure that the potentialities, aptitudes, aspirations and needs of women, including those living in rural areas, as well as those of men are taken fully into account in employment promotion programmes and strategies.

(5) Positive measures shall be taken to stimulate the equal access of women to top positions in both the public and the private sectors.

(6) So far as possible, jobs and workplaces shall be so designed as to be suitable for all workers, women as well as men.

Article 7

(1) Women workers shall be guaranteed the right to equal remuneration for work of equal value in accordance with the provisions of the Equal Remuneration Convention, 1951 (No. 100), and the Equal Remuneration Recommendation, 1951 (No. 90).

(2) Special measures shall be taken to ensure equal remuneration for work of equal value for women also in occupations in which women predominate and to measure the relative value of their work with full regard to the qualities essential to performing the job.

(3) Special measures shall be taken to raise the level of women's wages as compared with that of men's and to eradicate the causes of lower average earnings for women possessing the same or similar qualifications or doing the same work or work of equal value.

(4) Special measures shall be taken, as necessary and appropriate, to ensure equality of treatment for workers employed regularly on a part-time basis, the majority of whom are women, particularly with respect to pro rata fringe benefits.

Article 8

(1) There shall be no discrimination against women workers on the grounds of pregnancy and childbirth and women bearing a child shall be protected from dismissal on such grounds during the entire period of pregnancy and maternity leave. They shall have the right to resume their employment without loss of acquired rights.

(2) Adoptive parents shall also be entitled to time off to care for a child without losing the right to resume their employment or their acquired rights.

(3) Because maternity is a social function, all women workers shall be entitled to full maternity protection in line with the minimum standards set forth in the Maternity Protection Convention (Revised), 1952 (No. 103), and the Maternity Protection Recommendation, 1952 (No. 95), the costs of which should be borne by social security or other public funds or by means of collective arrangements.

(4) All couples and individuals have the basic right to decide freely and responsibly on the number and spacing of their children and to receive the necessary information, education and means to exercise this right.

Article 9

(1) Protection of women at work shall be an integral part of the efforts aimed at continuous promotion and improvement of living and working conditions of all employees.

(2) Women shall be protected from risks inherent in their employment and occupation on the same basis and with the same standards of protection as men, in the light of advances in scientific and technological knowledge.

(3) Studies and research shall be undertaken into processes which might have a harmful effect on women and men from the standpoint of their social function of reproduction.

Standards and policy statements of special interest to women workers

(4) Measures shall be taken to extend special protection to women for types of work proved to be harmful for them from the standpoint of their social function of reproduction and such measures shall be reviewed and brought up to date periodically in the light of advances in scientific and technological knowledge.

Article 10

In order to ensure practical equality of opportunity and treatment between men and women workers, all appropriate measures shall be taken to strengthen the social infrastructure and to provide the necessary supporting services and equipment in the community, in particular child-care and education services; such services and facilities shall be designed to meet the needs of children of all ages and the needs of their parents and shall be subsidised, run or supervised by the competent public authority.

Article 11

There shall be no discrimination against women in respect of social security and provisions concerning retirement and pensions, and differences in the treatment of men and women under such schemes shall be reviewed and revised.

Article 12

Review of the taxation system shall be considered wherever such system constitutes an obstacle to women's employment.

Article 13

In order to improve the status of women together with that of men in developing countries, special efforts shall be made to ensure that women, particularly in rural areas, are accorded an equitable share of all resources– national and international–available for development and that they are closely associated with development planning and implementation at the international, national and community levels.

Article 14

Equality of opportunity and treatment for women and men in working life shall be guaranteed by means of legislation, collective agreements or contractual arrangements of binding character. Measures shall be taken to enforce application of this principle, including procedures for complaints, conciliation, appeal and recourse to the courts.

Article 15

Members shall strengthen their national administrative machinery in order to give, together with employers' and workers' organisations, full effect to all measures aimed at preventing all forms of discrimination against women workers and at promoting and ensuring equality of opportunity and treatment for them.

Resolution concerning a Plan of Action with a View to Promoting Equality of Opportunity and Treatment for Women Workers, adopted by the International Labour Conference at its 60th Session (Geneva, 1975)

The General Conference of the International Labour Organisation,

Noting the obstacles still opposing the achievement of equality of opportunity and treatment for women workers,

Considering that sustained efforts must be made at the national, regional and international levels to overcome these obstacles and to enable women to enjoy full equality with men, without any discrimination with regard to employment and occupation, vocational training and conditions of life and work.

. . . .

Adopts the following Plan of Action with a view to ensuring the implementation of the principles set forth in the Declaration on Equality of Opportunity and Treatment for Women Workers.

FUNDAMENTAL PRINCIPLE

Any action aimed at establishing equality of opportunity and treatment of women workers must be determined on the basis of the fundamental principle that all human beings (men and women) have the undeniable right to work.

I. NATIONAL ACTION

1. General Policy

Member States should undertake to take specific action within the framework of national development planning to promote equality of opportunity and treatment for women workers in education, training, employment and occupation and to set up effective machinery, on a tripartite basis, and with the participation of women, for planning, stimulating and evaluating such action and for applying the policy of equal opportunity and treatment at all levels.

Standards and policy statements of special interest to women workers

2. Women's Participation in the Workforce

Measures should be taken to guarantee the right to work and to free choice of profession and occupation, and to fully integrate women on an equal basis and without discrimination in working life, including, specifically, measures appropriate in the national circumstances:

(a) to carry on a policy of economic and social development that will ensure full employment for women and men; and to open all employment opportunities for women by breaking down any barriers to women's employment in particular areas of work based on a sex-type division of labour or on the grounds of their marital status or age;

(b) to develop counselling, training and employment policies which take account of individual aptitudes, capacities and interests, irrespective of sex;

(c) to stimulate and create real opportunity for access of women to higher levels of skill and responsibility in the occupational structures;

(d) to analyse internal regional differences both in women's rate of activity and in the character of their participation in the workforce and take positive measures to provide equal work opportunities for both men and women in all regional development planning and action;

(e) to ensure adequate and appropriate attention to women's integration in work life in all national economic and social development planning and action;

(f) to ensure adequate and appropriate attention to all special categories of women who may encounter particular difficulties, such as migrant women who are frequently the victims of discrimination and exploitation and who also run social risks;

(g) to apply the same criteria to all workers in cases of redundancy or dismissal;

(h) to promote changes of attitudes towards the employment of women, irrespective of marital status or age (taking into account the provisions of Conventions and Recommendations dealing with minimum age of admission to employment), including the promotion of positive attitudes towards women's employment by employers and workers and their respective organisations, by men and women themselves and by society as a whole;

(i) to devote greater attention to women workers in the rural sector in order to promote fuller participation by such workers in the workforce and in national development.

3. Vocational Guidance and Training

Equality of opportunity and treatment for girls and women in respect of vocational guidance and training should be promoted to conform to the principles set forth in the relevant section of the Human Resources Development Recommendation, 1975, which reads as follows:

VIII. PROMOTION OF EQUALITY OF OPPORTUNITY OF WOMEN AND MEN IN TRAINING AND EMPLOYMENT

54. (1) Measures should be taken to promote equality of opportunity of women and men in employment and in society as a whole.

(2) These measures should form an integral part of all economic, social and cultural measures taken by governments for improving the employment situation of women and should include, as far as possible–

(a) educating the general public and in particular parents, teachers, vocational guidance and vocational training staff, the staff of employment and other social services, employers and workers, on the need for encouraging women and men to play an equal part in society and in the economy and for changing traditional attitudes regarding the work of women and men in the home and in working life;

(b) providing girls and women with vocational guidance on the same broad range of educational, vocational training and employment opportunities as boys and men, encouraging them to take full advantage of such opportunities and creating the conditions required for them to do so;

(c) promoting equality of access for girls and women to all streams of education and to vocational training for all types of occupations, including those which have been traditionally accessible only to boys and men, subject to the provisions of international labour Conventions and Recommendations;

(d) promoting further training for girls and women to ensure their personal development and advancement to skilled employment and posts of responsibility, and urging employers to provide them with the same opportunities of extending their work experience as offered to male workers with the same education and qualifications;

(e) providing day-care facilities and other services for children of different ages, in so far as possible, so that girls and women with family responsibilities have access to normal vocational training, as well as making special arrangements, for instance in the form of part-time or correspondence courses, vocational training programmes following a recurrent pattern or programmes using mass media;

(f) providing vocational training programmes for women above the normal age of entry into employment who wish to take up work for the first time or re-enter it after a period of absence.

55. Special vocational training arrangements and programmes, similar to those envisaged in clauses (e) and (f) of subparagraph (2) of Paragraph 54 of this Recommendation, should be available to men having analogous problems.

56. Account should be taken of the Employment Policy Convention and Recommendation, 1964, in the implementation of measures for the promotion of equality of opportunity of women and men in training and employment.

4. Promotion of Equality of Opportunity and Treatment in Employment and Occupation

All necessary measures should be taken:

(a) to ratify, as necessary, the Equal Remuneration Convention, 1951 (No. 100), the Discrimination (Employment and Occupation) Convention, 1958 (No. 111), and all other relevant Conventions of the ILO, in so far as they are concerned with sex discrimination. Workers' and employers' organisations should, through collective agreements or in other ways, assist in realising full implementation of the provisions of these instruments;

(b) to eliminate all forms of discrimination against women in all sectors of social and economic activity and at all levels of skill and responsibility;

(c) to ensure women's access to qualified employment in all sectors of economic and social activity and their in-service training;

(d) to promote, in particular, through government action, equal opportunities for women, such action to include legislation relating to equality of opportunity for women workers, and effective machinery under public control, for its enforcement; and to ensure strict application of the principle of non-discrimination in all sectors and especially those under public control;

(e) to create inter alia through educational and promotional activities, conducted in particular through the mass media and schools, social attitudes that are favourable to the employment of women including especially, married women and women with family responsibilities;

(f) to ensure that the right to work for women does not depend on the existing economic situation or on any other consideration and, therefore, that social measures for families are applied at all times without discrimination so that women are not discouraged from participation in economic life.

5. Social Security

Measures should be taken to eliminate all discriminatory treatment in social security schemes, in particular as concerns the payment of benefits, and to review the position of heads of families and single persons with regard to entitlement to social security benefits.

6. Review of Protective Legislation

Measures should be taken to review all protective legislation applying to women in the light of up-to-date scientific knowledge and technological advances and to revise, supplement, extend to all workers, retain, or repeal such legislation according to national circumstances, these measures being aimed at the improvement of the quality of life.

7. Right to Maternity Protection

All necessary measures should be adopted:

(a) in the light of scientific knowledge and technological advances, to extend the scope and to raise the standards of maternity protection, it being understood that the costs would be borne by social security or other public funds or by means of collective arrangements;

(b) to ensure that all couples and individuals have access to the necessary information, education and means to exercise their basic right to decide freely and responsibly on the number and spacing of their children;

(c) to make it possible for women workers to take leave for a reasonable time after the period of maternity leave without relinquishing their employment and all rights resulting from their employment being fully safeguarded.

8. Strengthening the Social Infrastructure

(1) In order to make women's right to work outside the home without discrimination fully effective in practice, measures should be taken along the lines laid down in the Employment (Women with Family Responsibilities) Recommendation, 1965 (No. 123), in particular:

(a) to adapt, as far as possible, working life to the needs of workers;

(b) to develop services and facilities meeting the needs of children of all ages and other dependants of workers, taking particular account of the migrant mother's need not to be separated from her children, regardless of her place of origin;

(c) to provide to all workers (men and women) information, assistance, community services and social amenities, to facilitate the harmonious combination of home and work responsibilities;

(d) to reduce household drudgery.

(2) Educational and promotional measures should be taken as necessary and appropriate to encourage a more equitable sharing among family members of household tasks, including child-rearing.

(3) Special attention should be given to the question of flexible working hours and of shorter working days for all workers where national circumstances permit, with a view to facilitating the harmonious accomplishment of family and work tasks and to promoting practical equality of opportunity and treatment for women workers.

9. Administrative Arrangements to Promote Equality of Opportunity and Treatment for Women Workers

Measures should be taken as necessary and appropriate:

(a) to establish a national tripartite commission on the status of women workers to direct action aimed at promoting equality of opportunity and treatment for women in economic and social life;

(b) to set up a central unit or appropriate administrative machinery which might serve as the secretariat of the national commission on the status of women workers. Such unit or machinery should develop and co-ordinate research and statistics, planning, programming and action on equality of opportunity and treatment for women workers, and disseminate knowledge and information pertaining to women's preparation for work life and their integration in the workforce, and provide a mechanism for systematic consultation with employers' and workers' organisations.

10. Women's Effective Participation in National, Regional and International Bodies

(1) The effective participation of women should be ensured in all national decision-making bodies, government commissions, advisory boards, councils, conferences and in all appropriate national and internal regional and community bodies.

(2) Measures should be taken to ensure that women are considered for and appointed to delegations on the same basis and by the same standards as men, whether to the International Labour Conference, to regional conferences of the ILO or to other national, regional and international meetings convened under the auspices of the ILO and other intergovernmental organisations.

11. General Measures

In order to ensure full equality of opportunity and treatment for women workers, measures should be taken to:

(a) achieve equality of opportunity and treatment for all workers in education, training, employment and occupation;
(b) change the still widely prevailing traditional attitudes of men and women to their role at work, in the family and in society.

III. ILO ACTION

1. Regional Action

Measures should be taken or envisaged to strengthen ILO action at the regional level with a view to promoting equality of opportunity and treatment for women workers, in particular:

(a) by placing the question of equality of opportunity and treatment for women workers on the agenda of future sessions of regional advisory committees and regional conferences;
(b) by studying the possibility of creating regional commissions on the status of women workers which will initiate regional and national programmes

of action for the advancement of women in economic, social and cultural life and the promotion of equality of opportunity and treatment for them and by strengthening the ILO's regional field structure so that these programmes can be implemented effectively and so that the ILO can co-operate closely on questions of importance to women at the regional level with other organisations of the United Nations system and with non-governmental organisations, especially employers' and workers' organisations;

(c) by promoting, in co-ordination with other bodies, in-depth studies on constraints on women's employment within different cultural and economic patterns and on possible means of relaxing or abolishing these constraints;

(d) by ensuring that ILO activities undertaken in the various regions, or its activities in co-operation with other United Nations agencies in connection with the World Employment Programme, or through technical co-operation projects, will promote the effective participation of women in development. Care should be taken to ensure that these activities do not lead to the perpetuation, maintenance or furthering of discrimination against women and to ensure the implementation of international labour standards, in particular Conventions Nos. 100, 103 and 111.

2. *International Action*

(1) The necessary measures should be taken with a view to furthering:

(a) the review and revision, if necessary, of ILO standards relating to the employment of women and other relevant instruments, including Conventions Nos. 100 and 111 and all protective instruments, in order to determine whether their provisions are still adequate in the light of experience acquired since their adoption and to keep them up to date in the light of scientific and technical knowledge and social progress;

(b) the development of new standards concerning discrimination on the basis of sex in areas not covered by existing standards and active promotion of equality *de facto* and *de jure.*

(2) Steps should be taken to initiate or strengthen research activities on problems of special interest to women, including those relating to the impact of technological progress on women's employment and conditions and to family care and planning and other aspects of the social infrastructure. As concerns the rural sector of developing countries, research activities should be initiated on the problems of poverty, illiteracy and lack of technical skill that have a direct bearing on women's employability and conditions of life and problems relating to family care and planning and other aspects of social infrastructure.

(3) Industrial Committees and analogous bodies should be invited to utilise a greater number of women experts, to give greater consideration to the position and problems of women within the industries concerned, and to

promote further participation by more women's representatives, particularly from economic sectors where women are employed in the majority.

(4) Measures should be taken to review the contribution and status of women workers in a changing world at the end of the Second Development Decade and the beginning of the Third Decade, for example, by providing for a Conference discussion in 1980 to evaluate progress made towards greater equality of opportunity and treatment for women workers in practice and to plan further action to this end.

(5) Measures should be taken by the International Labour Office to set an example in its own organisation so that any discrimination against women may be avoided and women may have equal opportunity of access to all posts. In addition, a unit of the International Labour Office should have the responsibility to study more closely the problems of women workers, to promote equality of opportunity and treatment for them, and to ensure that the needs of working women receive due attention in all aspects and all areas of the work of the Office, including employment, training, industrial relations, labour legislation and administration, social security and other related problems. The International Labour Organisation should also restructure and activate its existing tripartite body to promote equality of opportunity and treatment for women workers in the above-mentioned and other fields.

(6) The ILO, in conjunction with other bodies and experts of the countries concerned, should collect and analyse statistical and other data on women and men, pertaining both to developed and developing countries, such as are necessary for reviewing the status of women workers and measuring their total contribution to economic and social life.

Resolution concerning Equal Status and Equal Opportunity for Women and Men in Occupation and Employment adopted by the International Labour Conference at its 60th Session (Geneva, 1975)

The General Conference of the International Labour Organisation,

Considering the need for continued ILO action after the expiry of International Women's Year with a view to achieving progress in the direction of equal status and equal opportunities for women and men in occupation and employment, and a better working environment both for women and men;

1. Invites the Governing Body of the International Labour Office to instruct the Director-General–

(a) to study the need for new international instruments concerning equal opportunities and equal treatment for women and men in occupation and employment with a view to supplementing the provisions of the Equal Remuneration Convention, 1951 (No. 100), and the Discrimination (Employment and Occupation) Convention, 1958 (No. 111);[3]

(b) to carry out thorough and sufficiently extensive studies on matters relating to special protection for women and men as the case may be.

2. Invites the Governing Body—

(a) to call upon member States to supply reports under article 19 of the Constitution on the Maternity Protection Convention, 1919 (No. 3), the Maternity Protection Convention (Revised), 1952 (No. 103), and Part VIII (Maternity Benefits) of the Social Security (Minimum Standards) Convention, 1952 (No. 102), with a view to evaluating whether the provisions of these Conventions are adequate in the light of today's concept of the right to maternity protection;

(b) on the basis of the reports under article 19 of the Constitution to be supplied by member States in 1977 on the Employment (Women with Family Responsibilities) Recommendation, 1965 (No. 123), to place on the agenda of the earliest possible session of the International Labour Conference the question of workers with family responsibilities, with a view to the adoption of a new instrument.[4]

Texts adopted by ILO Regional Conferences

Resolution concerning Conditions of Work, Vocational Training and Employment of Women, adopted by the Eleventh Conference of American States Members of the ILO (Medellín, 1979)

The Eleventh Conference of American States Members of the International Labour Organisation,

Having met in Medellín (Colombia), from 26 September to 5 October 1979,
considering

1. That the contribution of women, both actual and potential, is indispensable to the achievement of greater economic and social development, of an increase in national income and thus greater and more equitable access to such income,

2. That the participation of women in the workforces of the Americas is increasing and that this has been accompanied by important qualitative changes, but that there is still a need for women to play a more active role in the economic and social development process, and to benefit more actively therefrom,

3. That in spite of this process, a series of problems persists which affect in particular certain specific groups of women workers: women in the traditional economy of rural areas, women in marginal urban areas employed mainly in the informal sector, and, in certain countries of the region, indigenous women.

4. That, moreover, the increased participation of women in the labour market may have adverse effects on the degree and quality of child care, due to inadequate social infrastructure in certain countries,

Standards and policy statements of special interest to women workers

5. That legal or institutional provisions regulating conditions of work for women should be established and applied on the same basis as for men workers, with the exception of the special protection accorded to women in view of the social function of maternity,

6. That discrimination which has a prejudicial effect on women persists despite their greater access to the education system, since at times qualifications superior to those required of men are demanded in order to fill the same occupational positions,

7. That, in addition, traditional forms of discrimination are still prevalent with regard to access to employment, as well as lower salaries for equal work and limited possibilities for access to posts at management and decision-making levels in enterprises, of public administration and of employers' and workers' organisations themselves.

8. That, in general, the value of domestic activity and work carried out by women in the home is not recognised, neither do women engaged in such tasks enjoy the direct protection of social security benefits pertaining to other labour activities,

9. That whereas it is true that the difficult situation confronting the woman of today springs fundamentally from causes outside her control, among which the most important is poverty, the obstacles she often faces in realising the full development of her intellectual capacity, and the fact that she is under-represented in the world of science and technology, often lead her to accept roles which downgrade her place in society and her personal development; that democratisation of education is based on equality of opportunities for the full development of individual potential and capacity and that formal and informal education, particularly vocational and technical training, is a factor which leads to the humanisation of work and a better society,

10. That the available statistics do not adequately reflect the actual and potential participation of women in economic life, owing principally to the inappropriateness of the categories used and of the usual means of measurement; that, in particular, female participation in rural areas is not adequately measured. And that any labour policies aimed at the elimination of preconceived ideas and of discrimination against female labour need to be based on actual, reliable data,

11. That the Constitution of the ILO states, in the second paragraph of the Preamble that "... whereas conditions of labour exist involving such injustice, hardship and privation to large numbers of people...", of whom a considerable number are women who are called upon to assume greater workloads and responsibilities; that the Universal Declaration of Human Rights proclaims the equality of all human beings and condemns all discrimination on grounds of sex, but that practice, customs, usages, and at times the laws themselves, do not respect these principles and tend to perpetuate the inferior status of women,

Basic human rights

12. That following the World Conference on International Women's Year (Mexico, 1975) and the proclamation of the period 1976–85 as the United Nations Decade for Women, the International Labour Organisation undertook to collaborate in the implementation of the World Plan of Action for the integration of women in the development process,

13. That the Tenth Session of the Conference of American States Members of the ILO (Mexico, 1974) adopted a resolution concerning ILO activities on behalf of women in the Americas; and that the 60th Session of the International Labour Conference (1975) adopted a resolution concerning a Plan of Action with a view to promoting equality of opportunity and treatment for women workers, and requested that this item be included on the agenda of future sessions of the regional advisory committees and regional conferences, that a study be made of the possibility of establishing regional commissions on the status of women workers, which would initiate regional and national programmes of action for the advancement of women in economic, social and cultural life and the promotion of equality of opportunity and treatment for them, and that the ILO's regional field structure be strengthened to that effect.

14. That the Governing Body decided to place on the agenda of the 66th Session of the International Labour Conference (1980), in accordance with the recommendation contained in the resolution concerning the ILO's plan of action, the subject: equality of opportunity and treatment of men and women workers; workers with family responsibilities. That the ILO is well placed to co-operate at the regional level, on questions relating to women, with other organisations of the United Nations system and with non-governmental organisations, particularly workers' and employers' organisations.

recommends

Fundamental Principle

1. That any action aimed at establishing equality of opportunity and treatment of women workers must be determined on the basis of the fundamental principle that all human beings (men and women) have the undeniable right to work.

Employment Policy

2. That the employment policies of the countries of the region should pay special attention to disadvantaged groups, principally the rural traditional sector, the informal urban sector and the indigenous sector, given the high concentration of women in these sectors, in order to implement the recommendations of the World Employment Conference of 1976 which have been reiterated recently during the last International Labour Conference.

Standards and policy statements of special interest to women workers

*Assistance in the Discharge of Home
and Family Responsibilities*

3. That governments should establish and apply standards, appropriate to national conditions, which would allow for the creation and extension of child-care centres, with locations and timetables convenient for home and work, and responding to the schedules of workers with family responsibilities.

4. That housing plans should envisage the creation of community services which would facilitate domestic work.

Change of Attitudes

5. That by extensive information campaigns, modifications in the form and content of education and the dissemination of knowledge concerning the rights and obligations of working women, among other means, changes should be encouraged in the attitudes of men and women with respect to domestic and social functions.

6. That as regards cultural and social policies American States Members of the ILO should intensify action designed to change material conditions and mental attitudes with a view to enhancing the value of women as individuals entitled to personal development, on the basis of independence and of their integration into society as an essential element for national development.

Maternity Protection

7. That the financing of special protection for the working mother should not involve costs directly related to her employment, which could result in discrimination in her engagement or stability of employment; to avoid this, revisions of existing systems of financing would be desirable.

Social Security

8. That social security provisions should be applied in a manner that will not imply discrimination against women, particularly as regards survivors' pension in favour of the spouse, and the elimination of drawbacks related to the interruption of their working life and the resulting limitation of benefits. Moreover, that special attention should be paid to the manner in which women performing paid work at home, domestic workers, and those engaged in household duties living in rural areas and in urban marginal areas, could be incorporated into social security schemes.

Labour Legislation

9. That measures should be taken to revise and supplement where necessary, in the light of up-to-date scientific knowledge, technological advan-

Basic human rights

ces and international Conventions, the protective legislation applying specifically to women with the object of ensuring that this does not produce discrimination in treatment.

Discrimination

10. That, with the object of achieving equality, the wider and active participation of women in employers' and workers' organisations, or other forms of association, should be promoted.

11. That all necessary measures should be taken to ratify the Equal Remuneration Convention, 1951 (No. 100), the Discrimination (Employment and Occupation) Convention, 1958 (No. 111), and all other relevant Conventions of the ILO concerned with sex discrimination with a view to ensuring their full application. Workers' and employers' organisations should, through collective agreements or in other ways, take the necessary measures to achieve full implementation of the provisions of these instruments.

Education and Vocational Training

12. That governments and workers' and employers' organisations should promote equality of access for women to all types and levels of education and training for all classes of employment, including those which have been traditionally accessible only to men; that such promotion should pay special attention to vocational training for rural groups, the marginal urban sector and indigenous groups.

Statistical Measurement

13. That measurement categories should be revised with the object of collecting more precise information on the participation of the disadvantaged sectors, with special reference to women; to evaluate in statistical terms the activities carried out by women in the home, and to adopt adequate criteria for the measurement of female employment in the rural sector in order to assess the effective contribution of work carried out within family surroundings; that existing means of measurement, in particular censuses and household surveys, should incorporate these revisions.

Valuation

14. That, as awareness grows of the social contribution which household tasks carried out by women in the home represent, measures should be adopted to assess the value of such tasks.

ILO Action

15. That the ILO should collaborate with governments, workers and employers, in order to put into effect the foregoing recommendations. That,

in particular, the ILO should strengthen the work being carried out in the region by the Inter-American Vocational Training Research and Documentation Centre (CINTERFOR), aimed at encouraging and upgrading training schemes for workers, particularly for women workers in the region; that, moreover, the ILO should promote programmes and projects for the training and skill development of women in all sectors of society, with particular reference to the contribution which women can make through the full utilisation of their capacities, creativity and intelligence; and that through the Regional Employment Programme for Latin America and the Caribbean (PREALC), the ILO should promote an employment programme which would include, as a special strategy, the development of the labour factor, in particular that of female labour.

16. That the ILO should continue to accord priority attention to the implementation of the recommendations contained in the Plan of Action for women of 1975 and that of the World Employment Conference of 1976; that the ILO should collaborate in the analysis of means of financing maternity protection, in the revision of the legal standards in force in each country and in the provision of adequate vocational training schemes.

17. That the ILO should accelerate its work in the region in the field of investigations and studies relating to women, in particular concerning those factors which determine the conditions and characteristics of the supply and demand for female labour, with a view to undertaking concrete measures to encourage increased participation of women through the promotion of employment and training; in particular, the ILO should continue to co-operate, through research and technical co-operation, in the analysis of the conditions of life and work of disadvantaged groups, and in the implementation of programmes designed to benefit them.

18. That the ILO should intensify efforts aimed at improving the statistical measurement of the economic participation of such groups; particularly that, in consultation with member States, it should draw up statistical concepts and criteria which would guide those responsible for carrying out censuses and surveys, in accordance with national circumstances, and thus lead to uniformity of procedures in the evaluation of female participation in the labour force.

19. That the ILO should prepare a report which would establish clearly the extent to which women are covered by social security provisions in respect of *(a)* sickness, *(b)* maternity, *(c)* family allowances, and *(d)* old-age, invalidity and survivors' pensions, for each of the American States Members of the ILO. This report should provide statistical data on the proportion of the female population covered by social security and the means of financing these benefits, showing the contributions of the employer, the worker and the State.

20. That the ILO should undertake studies with a view to defining the economic value of household activities in the countries of the region; that

such studies should form the basis for considering protective measures similar to those applicable to other labour sectors which receive due evaluation and effective protection.

21. That a forthcoming session of the International Labour Conference should have before it draft regulatory instruments on the subject, so that by means of Conventions, Recommendations or resolutions, governments may be encouraged to include in the national legislation the defence of the rights of women.

Resolution concerning the Employment and Conditions of Work of Women in African Countries, adopted by the Second African Regional Conference (Addis Ababa, 1964)

The Second African Regional Conference of the International Labour Organisation,

Conscious of the increasingly important role played by women in economic and social life in African countries,

Conscious also of the fact that the employment patterns and ways of work and life are undergoing a profound transformation which will have a significant influence on the future of Africa as a whole,

Considering the importance of integrating women fully and effectively in the whole development process and of raising their status through measures aimed at enabling them to assume still greater responsibilities in relation to the economic, social and cultural development of their countries,

Recognising the need to respect changing social attitudes relating to women's employment outside the home,

. . . .

Adopts the following resolution and recommends the Governing Body of the International Labour Office to transmit it to the African States Members of the International Labour Organisation in order that they may take account of the considerations and apply the principles and measures set forth therein in connection with the employment and conditions of work of women as rapidly as national conditions allow.

1. Within the framework of national economic and social development and of planning employment expansion, particular efforts should be made to widen and to diversify the employment opportunities available to girls and women in both urban and rural areas. Such efforts should include a sustained campaign amongst employers in the public and private sectors aimed at drawing their attention to the potentialities of women as workers, and a planned development of further opportunities for women to work on their own account, e.g. in handicraft and cottage industries. In view of continuing shortages of specific types of trained workers in many occupations which are

as suitable for women as for men or more so, development plans should make full and appropriate provision for the best use of womanpower as well as for the best use of manpower.

2. Since the recognised outstanding need of girls and women throughout Africa is for more schooling, national educational plans should take full account of the urgent need–

(a) to expand educational facilities in general and to provide adequate facilities for girls as well as boys;
(b) to give girls full access to the available facilities;
(c) to educate parents in the desirability of giving the same importance to the education of their girls as to that of their boys;
(d) to get girls to start school at the normal school age; and
(e) to educate girls themselves to appreciate the practical significance of their future work lives and of their economic and social advancement generally.

The education provided for girls should be of the same level and quality as that provided for boys.

3. In order to assist in making effective use of the talents and abilities of girls and women seeking gainful employment, steps should be taken, if necessary by stages or by areas, to bring employment information to school leavers and to develop realistic vocational guidance for girls and women, helping them to an understanding of their capabilities, the practical need for women workers and the work opportunities available and the preparation required.

4. Action should be taken to expand vocational training opportunities for girls and women in accordance with immediate and foreseeable national manpower requirements. In this connection measures are needed–

(a) for the training of girls and women with little or no formal education, including measures and facilities for the adequate vocational training of girls and women in "home" or "cottage" industries and for agricultural occupations (e.g. through mobile instruction services), in catering, hotel work and various forms of domestic service employment and in certain types of factory work which do not require any special educational qualifications;
(b) for the training of women with some degree of formal education to prepare them for varied types of employment, including factory and office work, all other employments equally suitable for men and women, and employment as welfare workers with big employers, as well as for management and supervisory work;
(c) for the technical and professional training of women and the encouragement of wider opportunities for the training of such highly qualified women;

(d) for the supervision and control by public authority of private agencies or institutions providing vocational training for girls and women, in order to ensure their efficiency.

5. Simultaneously with the progressive development of training facilities for these purposes, special measures should be taken within the framework of community development to encourage girls and women to make optimum use of the training opportunities open to them and to provide them with equal access to the facilities available at the various levels.

6. Measures should be taken to include women in courses organised, according to the needs of the country, for the training of vocational instructors.

7. In order to develop training on a sound technical basis, and in order to promote recognition of agreed standards of qualifications in the different occupations of particular interest from the standpoint of women's employment, measures should be taken to establish such standards for certain occupations and to issue uniform and nationally valid certificates of qualification on successful completion of the necessary training.

8. Women seeking work should receive adequate and appropriate attention within the framework of the employment exchanges or services. In this connection, consideration should be given to the establishment of specialised sections for women, staffed by qualified officials. Moreover, women should be trained in adequate numbers for more general aspects of employment service work, e.g. for youth employment work and for vocational guidance work, including aptitude testing.

9. The structure of social protection for women should be kept under continuous and systematic review, with a view to ensuring that it is adequate and up to date and responds effectively to the changing needs of women in rural and urban areas in the process of economic and social development. Care must be taken to ensure that legislation applying to women meets their needs satisfactorily, particularly as regards their safety, health and welfare, but without unduly infringing, their employment opportunities. Appropriate action should be taken to extend social legislation as rapidly as possible to women working in sectors of the economy not yet covered by such protection, including the self-employed.

10. In this connection, special attention should be given to improving and extending the enforcement of all labour laws, including those especially affecting women, with particular emphasis on the enforcement of safety and health legislation.

11. Appropriate numbers of women should be included in the initial and further training provided for labour inspectors (including factory inspectors), and women should be appointed to and advanced in labour inspection work according to their qualifications.

12. Application of the principle of equal remuneration for men and women workers for work of equal value should be encouraged.

13. Maternity protection schemes should be established where they do not already exist and should be kept under review to ensure their extension to women not yet covered, including the self-employed, and their adequacy in terms of the protection afforded and their implications for the employment, welfare and well-being of women and the welfare and well-being of their children. Particular importance should be attached to the provision, on as wide a scale as possible, of free medical care for all women before, during and after childbirth.

14. Women should be entitled to join trade unions of their choice freely and should have the possibility of occupying responsible posts in the unions and of obtaining adequate training for this purpose.

15. Measures should be taken to improve the conditions of self-employed women and to ensure that they are provided with the amenities and facilities needed to make their daily work tolerable and dignified. Since co-operatives form an important means of protecting women from exploitation in many kinds of work, particularly agricultural work and home and cottage industries, the sound development of co-operatives should be encouraged and women should be given opportunities to learn about co-operative organisation and management and to take part in courses for training co-operative leaders.

16. More adequate and suitable provision should be made as a matter of urgency, within the limits of national possibilities, for the care of the children of working women, taking account so far as possible of the latter's preferences as regards facilities suitable for children of different ages, and appropriate training should be provided for the personnel who are engaged in infant and child care.

17. In the larger communities where women are going out to work, whether wage-earning or not, in greater numbers and in difficult circumstances, the arrangements for meeting their other practical day-to-day needs should be studied carefully, with a view to improving existing conditions. In this connection special efforts should be made to provide hostels for girls and young women living away from home and also to provide other forms of accommodation suitable for working women. Steps should also be taken to improve public transport, which has a special relevance to the problems of women workers who can ill afford the time added to their burden of work, at home and outside it, by inadequate means of transportation. Finally, measures should be taken wherever possible to promote the progressive extension of practical conveniences to facilitate household work, such as labour-saving devices. These should be available for purchase at reasonable prices by individuals, or by groups such as co-operatives or communities, or public authorities should install them in central positions, in housing projects or communities, to be used by women in exchange for a small fee.

Basic human rights

18. In dealing with many of the problems of women's employment, the services of social workers and of voluntary organisations should be enlisted as may be necessary and appropriate.

19. In the consideration and formulation of policy regarding the employment of women there should be consultation and co-operation between public authorities and employers' and workers' organisations at all appropriate levels. Women representatives should take part in consultations to the maximum extent possible.

20. In view of the special importance of ILO standards relating to the employment and conditions of work of women, particularly those concerned with maternity protection, safety and health, the regulation of night work, equal remuneration for work of equal value and non-discrimination in employment and occupation, every effort should be made to ensure the early ratification and full implementation of these standards.

Resolution concerning ILO Action to Advance the Economic and Social Status of Women in African Countries, adopted by the Second African Regional Conference (Addis Ababa, 1964)

The Second African Regional Conference of the International Labour Organisation,

. . . .

Conscious of the need for international co-operation in advancing the economic and social status of women in African countries,

Aware of the importance of the role of the International Labour Organisation in this connection,

. . . .

Urgently appeals to the Governing Body of the International Labour Office to find the ways and means whereby the International Labour Organisation may intensify its work on behalf of women on the African continent and in particular urges that the programme of work of the International Labour Organisation in this region should include action along the following lines:

1. The International Labour Organisation, in co-operation with other organisations as appropriate, should do everything in its power to facilitate the international exchange of information and experience among women within Africa, in view of the practical importance of this interchange from the standpoint of their economic and social advancement. To this end it might help to organise for women in African countries, and with their active participation, interregional seminars and workshops organised around particular problems or topics of special concern to them, and should help to organise individual training, study and work visits.

Standards and policy statements of special interest to women workers

2. The International Labour Organisation should expand its technical co-operation activities in fields of special interest to women in African countries and at the same time should ensure that in all technical co-operation projects, e.g. manpower surveys and surveys of training needs, training projects of all kinds and handicraft and cottage industry projects, full account is taken of women workers' needs as well as those of men.

3. The International Labour Organisation, on request, should assist governments to carry out, in consultation with employers' and workers' organisations, surveys of women workers' needs and practical field studies on women workers' problems within the African region, with a view to throwing light on the changes occurring with economic development and the implications of these changes for the employment and conditions of work of women in Africa. It should also continue to assist governments in appraising and forecasting their general requirements for workers at all levels in all fields, with a view to throwing light on women's employment opportunities and training needs.

4. The International Labour Organisation should encourage governments to include suitable women amongst candidates for study abroad and fellowships of other kinds.

5. The International Labour Organisation's manpower, employment creation and rural development programmes should include projects aimed specifically at raising the economic and social status and improving the conditions of work of women in African countries.

6. The workers' education programme of the International Labour Organisation should devote particular attention to the needs and problems of women workers in Africa. Apart from assistance to seminars, it might also be useful to develop a special manual on the employment and conditions of work of women which could be helpful in meeting the needs and problems of women in African countries as well as elsewhere.

7. The International Labour Organisation should do its utmost to assign suitable African women experts to the various countries in the region.

8. Since many of the problems of women workers are interrelated, and since a many-sided approach to them is necessary, the International Labour Organisation should continue to work in the closest co-operation with the United Nations, and particularly its regional Economic Commission for Africa and its Commission on the Status of Women, the Food and Agriculture Organisation of the United Nations, the World Health Organisation, the United Nations Educational, Scientific and Cultural Organisation and other international and regional organisations concerned, with a view to intensifying co-ordinated international efforts for the advancement of women within the context of African development.

Basic human rights

Texts adopted by ILO Industrial Meetings, etc.

Conclusions (No. 72) concerning the Forecasting of Manpower Requirements in the Iron and Steel Industry and its Significance for the Recruitment and Vocational Training of the Industry's Labour Force, adopted by the Iron and Steel Committee at its Ninth Session (Geneva, 1975)

. . . .

General Considerations

. . . .

2. Within the framework of manpower requirements, equality of access to employment and training, irrespective of race, colour, sex, religion, political opinion, national extraction or social origin, should be ensured by governments, with the collaboration of employers' and workers' organisations.

. . . .

Recruitment and Selection

. . . .

18. Before proceeding to external recruitment, every effort should be made to use internal resources by transfer and/or promotion and to give each person the opportunity to rise to the highest position which he or she is capable of filling.

. . . .

21. The Committee recognises without any reservations that women must have the opportunity to work in the iron and steel industry and receive equal pay for work of equal value.

. . . .

Training

. . . .

28. Training programmes should be conceived to meet the immediate and future employment needs of the iron and steel industry as well as those of the individual. Training programmes should therefore aim at developing a person's occupational capabilities and fulfilling his or her occupational aspirations.

. . . .

Conclusions (No. 71) concerning Conditions of Work and Life of Employees in Commerce and Offices, adopted by the Advisory Committee on Salaried Employees and Professional Workers at its Seventh Session (Geneva, 1974)

. . . .

Special Problems of Women Employees

43. It is to be noted with satisfaction that a number of international instruments exist which are designed to ensure adequate social protection for

women workers, and their ratification and effective application should be encouraged.

44. However, much still remains to be done in practice to ensure equality of rights and opportunities for women employees in the different aspects of conditions of work and life and in employment, vocational training, further training, retraining, promotion, protection for pregnant women and protection against disadvantages due to interruption of working life for family reasons.

45. The practical application of this equality of rights and opportunities concerns employers as well as workers and governments and evolution of attitudes is equally indispensable for the effective application of the principles concerned.

46. It would be useful to study the means of best dealing with the problems caused by the existence of family responsibilities when the mother works and, in particular, special leave arrangements for parents having such responsibilities, as well as the problem of re-entry of women into working life after an interruption of it.

. . . .

Compendium of Principles and Good Practices relating to the Conditions of Work and Employment of Professional Workers, adopted by the Tripartite Meeting on Conditions of Work and Employment of Professional Workers (Geneva, 1977)

. . . .

Employment

11. A policy designed, in accordance with the Employment Policy Convention, 1964 (No. 122), to ensure to all professional workers, without discrimination, jobs that are freely chosen and that correspond to their qualifications and aspirations should be placed in the broader context of a full employment policy for all.

. . . .

Equal Opportunities between Men and Women

50. Women and men should have the right on the same terms to receive education and training for highly qualified jobs.

51. The public authorities, and in particular the school and vocational guidance services, should systematically inform young people of both sexes so that they choose the types of training most likely to offer good prospects of employment and career development.

52. Women and men should enjoy equality of opportunity and treatment for career advancement.

53. The public authorities, in co-operation with employers' and workers' organisations and educational and training institutions, should

establish services to give advice and guidance to highly qualified women desiring to resume work after a break in employment. Such women should have access to appropriate training facilities for the updating of their knowledge or the acquisition of new qualifications.

. . . .

Conclusions (No. 2) concerning Employment Security in Civil Aviation, adopted by the Tripartite Technical Meeting for Civil Aviation (Geneva, 1977)

. . . .

Protection against Discrimination

9. Women and men should have equality of treatment in accordance with the principles set out in the Discrimination (Employment and Occupation) Convention, 1958 (No. 111).

. . . .

Conclusions on the Effects of Technological Changes on Conditions of Work and Employment in Postal and Telecommunications Services, adopted by the Joint Meeting on Conditions of Work and Employment in Postal and Telecommunications Services (Geneva, 1977)

. . . .

3. Contemplated mechanisation or technological changes should not provide any basis for discrimination because of race, colour, creed, religion, national origin, sex, age or marital status, or because of a physical handicap with respect to a position the duties of which can be performed efficiently by any individual so handicapped and without danger to his own health or safety or that of others.

. . . .

29. Staff structures should be reviewed and modified as appropriate in the context of technological changes to provide improved career opportunities wherever possible. Special attention should also be given to ensuring that women enjoy the same career opportunities as men.

. . . .

EQUAL REMUNERATION FOR MEN AND WOMEN[5]

Texts adopted by the International Labour Conference

(1) Equal Remuneration Convention, 1951 (No. 100)

. . . .

Article 1

For the purpose of this Convention–

(a) the term "remuneration" includes the ordinary, basic or minimum wage

or salary and any additional emoluments whatsoever payable directly or indirectly, whether in cash or in kind, by the employer to the worker and arising out of the worker's employment;

(b) the term "equal remuneration for men and women workers for work of equal value" refers to rates of remuneration established without discrimination based on sex.

Article 2

1. Each Member shall, by means appropriate to the methods in operation for determining rates of remuneration, promote and, in so far as is consistent with such methods, ensure the application to all workers of the principle of equal remuneration for men and women workers for work of equal value.

2. This principle may be applied by means of–

(a) national laws or regulations;
(b) legally established or recognised machinery for wage determination;
(c) collective agreements between employers and workers; or
(d) a combination of these various means.

Article 3

1. Where such action will assist in giving effect to the provisions of this Convention measures shall be taken to promote objective appraisal of jobs on the basis of the work to be performed.

2. The methods to be followed in this appraisal may be decided upon by the authorities responsible for the determination of rates of remuneration, or, where such rates are determined by collective agreements, by the parties thereto.

3. Differential rates between workers which correspond, without regard to sex, to differences, as determined by such objective appraisal, in the work to be performed shall not be considered as being contrary to the principle of equal remuneration for men and women workers for work of equal value.

. . . .

(1) Equal Remuneration Recommendation, 1951 (No. 90)

. . . .

1. Appropriate action should be taken, after consultation with the workers' organisations concerned or, where such organisations do not exist, with the workers concerned–

(a) to ensure the application of the principle of equal remuneration for men and women workers for work of equal value to all employees of central Government departments or agencies; and

(b) to encourage the application of the principle to employees of State, provincial or local government departments or agencies, where these have jurisdiction over rates of remuneration.

2. Appropriate action should be taken, after consultation with the employers' and workers' organisations concerned, to ensure, as rapidly as practicable, the application of the principle of equal remuneration for men and women workers for work of equal value in all occupations, other than those mentioned in Paragraph 1, in which rates of remuneration are subject to statutory regulation or public control, particularly as regards—

(a) the establishment of minimum or other wage rates in industries and services where such rates are determined under public authority;

(b) industries and undertakings operated under public ownership or control; and

(c) where appropriate, work executed under the terms of public contracts.

3. (1) Where appropriate in the light of the methods in operation for the determination of rates of remuneration, provision should be made by legal enactment for the general application of the principle of equal remuneration for men and women workers for work of equal value.

(2) The competent public authority should take all necessary and appropriate measures to ensure that employers and workers are fully informed as to such legal requirements and, where appropriate, advised on their application.

4. When, after consultation with the organisations of workers and employers concerned, where such exist, it is not deemed feasible to implement immediately the principle of equal remuneration for men and women workers for work of equal value, in respect of employment covered by Paragraphs 1, 2 or 3, appropriate provision should be made or caused to be made, as soon as possible, for its progressive application, by such measures as—

(a) decreasing the differentials between rates of remuneration for men and rates of remuneration for women for work of equal value;

(b) where a system of increments is in force, providing equal increments for men and women workers performing work of equal value.

5. Where appropriate for the purpose of facilitating the determination of rates or remuneration in accordance with the principle of equal remuneration for men and women workers for work of equal value, each Member should, in agreement with the employers' and workers' organisations concerned, establish or encourage the establishment of methods for objective appraisal of the work to be performed, whether by job analysis or by other procedures, with a view to providing a classification of jobs without regard to sex; such methods should be applied in accordance with the provisions of Article 2 of the Convention.

6. In order to facilitate the application of the principle of equal remuneration for men and women workers for work of equal value, appropri-

ate action should be taken, where necessary, to raise the productive efficiency of women workers by such measures as–

(a) ensuring that workers of both sexes have equal or equivalent facilities for vocational guidance or employment counselling, for vocational training and for placement;

(b) taking appropriate measures to encourage women to use facilities for vocational guidance or employment counselling, for vocational training and for placement;

(c) providing welfare and social services which meet the needs of women workers, particularly those with family responsibilities, and financing such services from general public funds or from social security or industrial welfare funds financed by payments made in respect of workers without regard to sex; and

(d) promoting equality of men and women workers as regards access to occupations and posts without prejudice to the provisions of international regulations and of national laws and regulations concerning the protection of the health and welfare of women.

7. Every effort should be made to promote public understanding of the grounds on which it is considered that the principle of equal remuneration for men and women workers for work of equal value should be implemented.

8. Such investigations as may be desirable to promote the application of the principle should be undertaken.

Text adopted by an ILO Regional Conference

Resolution concerning Remuneration, adopted by the Ninth Conference of American States Members of the ILO (Caracas, 1970)

The Ninth Conference of American States Members of the International Labour Organisation,

. . . .

Considering that the inequalities in the wages and social benefits enjoyed by the workers of the American countries contribute to economic instability, and that their influence on general economic development should be examined,

. . . .

1. Urges each country of the Americas, within the framework of over-all policies for economic and social development, to adopt wage policies that apply to all workers without discrimination.

2. Stresses that the following principles should be fully observed and applied in devising and implementing such wage policies:

. . . .

Basic human rights

(b) the integration of wage policies into broader policies covering all other types of incomes;

. . . .

(d) equal pay for work of equal value.

. . . .

Texts adopted by ILO Industrial Meetings, etc.

Resolution (No. 63) concerning the Wages of Women Employed in the Textile Industry, adopted by the Textiles Committee at its 8th Session (Geneva, 1968)

. . . .

Considering that in many countries the textile labour force includes a majority of women workers,

Noting that these women workers are usually employed in the lower-paid processes which, combined with the fact that many ILO member States have not yet ratified or implemented the Equal Remuneration Convention, 1951 (No. 100), diminishes the attractiveness of the textiles industry to young women workers,

. . . .

The Textiles Committee invites the Governing Body to request the Director-General to draw the attention of ILO member States to the advisability of eliminating unjustifiable differences between men's and women's wages.

Conclusions (No. 57) concerning the Impact of Social and Economic Developments on Working and Living Conditions in the Distributive Trades, adopted by the Advisory Committee on Salaried Employees and Professional Workers at its 6th Session (Geneva, 1967)

. . . .

Remuneration

70. Salaries of distributive workers should be comparable to salaries paid in other occupations requiring similar or equivalent qualifications and they should provide those workers with the means to ensure a reasonable standard of living for themselves and their families.

72. The salary structure should be planned so as not to give rise to injustices or anomalies tending to lead to friction between different categories of distributive workers.

73. Salary differentials should be based on objective criteria such as levels of qualification, years of experience or degrees of responsibility but the relationship between the lowest and the highest salary should be of a reasonable order.

Standards and policy statements of special interest to women workers

74. Particular attention should be given to the application of the fundamental principle laid down in the Equal Remuneration Convention, 1951 (No. 100), so as to ensure women workers equality of opportunity and treatment in employment in the distributive trades.

. . . .

76. Salary scales for distributive workers should be reviewed periodically to take account of factors such as a rise in the cost of living, changes in the pattern and methods of operation, increased productivity leading to higher standards of living in the country or a general upward movement in wage or salary levels.

. . . .

Conclusions (No. 71) concerning Conditions of Work and Life of Employees in Commerce and Offices, adopted by the Advisory Committee on Salaried Employees and Professional Workers at its Seventh Session (Geneva, 1974)

. . . .

REMUNERATION

. . . .

4. Remuneration should be fixed on the basis of such objective criteria as level of qualifications, degree of responsibility, job requirements, nature of the work and length of service, and the difference between the lowest and the highest salary should be kept within reasonable limits.

5. Equal pay for work of equal value should be assured in accordance with the provisions of the Equal Remuneration Convention, 1951 (No. 100), which should be ratified as widely as possible. Care should be taken to establish and apply methods for objective appraisal of the work to be performed with a view to providing a classification of jobs without regard to sex, as laid down in the Equal Remuneration Recommendation, 1951 (No. 90).

. . . .

Conclusions (No. 1) concerning Conditions of Work in the Clothing Industry adopted by the Tripartite Technical Meeting for the Clothing Industry (Geneva, 1964)

. . . .

Remuneration of Women Workers

24. The problem of the remuneration of women workers is of great importance in view of the large proportion of women engaged in the clothing industry. It is particularly desirable to apply the principles laid down in the Equal Remuneration Convention, 1951. For this purpose it would be useful to establish job classifications based on a rational evaluation of the work to be carried out without distinction of sex.

Basic human rights

25. In a fairly large number of countries the clothing industry is characterised by a traditional distinction between men's and women's jobs, by which certain occupations are performed only by women and paid for at rates which yield lower wages than do jobs which are of a comparable level of skill and which are generally performed by men. Appropriate measures should be taken to enable women workers to enjoy equal opportunities and remuneration in accordance with the principles set out in the Discrimination (Employment and Occupation) Convention, 1958, wherein it is made clear that special measures for protection or for assistance provided for by other Conventions or Recommendations adopted by the International Labour Conference are not deemed to constitute discrimination.

. . . .

Conclusions (No. 2) concerning Conditions of Employment for the Leather and Footwear Industry, adopted by the Tripartite Technical Meeting for the Leather and Footwear Industry (Geneva, 1969)

. . . .

7. Continuous efforts should be made to establish a rational and fair wage structure with no serious discrepancies, such as shall facilitate the recruitment, training and stabilisation of the workforce and encourage the advanced training of workers. In establishing the wage structure, account should be taken, among other factors, of the conditions, difficulties and hazards of each job, and the level of occupational skill, experience, degree of initiative and responsibility required.

8. The problem of fair remuneration for women workers is of great importance because of the high proportion of women employed in the industry. It would be especially desirable for all countries to ratify the Equal Remuneration Convention, 1951 (No. 100), and for the principles laid down in the Convention to be effectively applied. In order to ensure equal remuneration for equal work, the causes of discrimination in employment, job classification and promotion should be removed.

. . . .

Notes

[1] Similar provisions are contained in Paragraph 1 of the Discrimination (Employment and Occupation) Recommendation, 1958 (No. 111), below.

[2] The Social Policy (Basic Aims and Standards) Convention, 1962 (No. 117), revised the Social Policy (Non-Metropolitan Territories) Convention, 1947 (No. 82), primarily with a view to making its continued application and ratification possible for independent States.

[3] The Governing Body at its 209th (February-March 1979) Session decided to include in category 4 (possible subjects for new instruments) the question of "Equal opportunities and equal treatment for men and women in employment and occupation". One aspect of this, namely "equal opportunities and equal treatment for men and women workers: workers with family responsibilities", has been placed on the agenda of the 66th (1980) Session of the Conference for first discussion.

Standards and policy statements of special interest to women workers

[4] See footnote under the Employment (Women with Family Responsibilities) Recommendation, 1965 (No. 123), in the Section: Facilities and Services for Women Workers with Family Responsibilities.

[5] See also under "Elimination of discrimination against women and promotion of equality of treatment for them in employment and related matters".

EMPLOYMENT POLICY AND HUMAN RESOURCES DEVELOPMENT 2

EMPLOYMENT POLICY

Texts adopted by the International Labour Conference

(1) Employment Policy Convention, 1964 (No. 122)

. . . .

Article 1[1]

1. With a view to stimulating economic growth and development, raising levels of living, meeting manpower requirements and overcoming unemployment and underemployment, each Member shall declare and pursue, as a major goal, an active policy designed to promote full, productive and freely chosen employment.

2. The said policy shall aim at ensuring that–

(a) there is work for all who are available for and seeking work;

(b) such work is as productive as possible;

(c) there is freedom of choice of employment and the fullest possible opportunity for each worker to qualify for, and to use his skills and endowments in, a job for which he is well suited, irrespective of race, colour, sex, religion, political opinion, national extraction or social origin.

3. The said policy shall take due account of the stage and level of economic development and the mutual relationships between employment objectives and other economic and social objectives, and shall be pursued by methods that are appropriate to national conditions and practices.

. . . .

(1) Employment Policy Recommendation, 1964 (No. 122)

. . . .

29. (1) Employers and workers in the public and private sectors, and their organisations, should take all practicable measures to promote the achievement and maintenance of full, productive and freely chosen employment.

(2) In particular, they should–

. . . .

(g) respect the principle of equality of opportunity and treatment in employment and occupation, taking account of the provisions of the Discrimination (Employment and Occupation) Convention and Recommendation, 1958.

. . . .

(1) Employment Service Recommendation, 1948 (No. 83)

. . . .

4. Measures should be taken in appropriate cases to develop, within the general framework of the employment services–

. . . .

(c) adequate arrangements for the placement of women on the basis of their occupational skill and physical capacity.

. . . .

12. The employment service should–

. . . .

(c) not, in referring workers to employment, itself discriminate against applicants on grounds of race, colour, sex or belief.

. . . .

(1) Special Youth Schemes Recommendation, 1970 (No. 136)

. . . .

1. (1) This Recommendation applies to special schemes designed to enable young persons to take part in activities directed to the economic and social development of their country and to acquire education, skills and experience facilitating their subsequent economic activity on a lasting basis and promoting their participation in society.

. . . .

5. Special schemes should be administered without discrimination on the basis of race, colour, sex, religion, political opinion, national extraction or social origin; they should be used for the active promotion of equality of opportunity and treatment.

. . . .

16. The content of special schemes should be adapted to and may vary, even within one scheme, according to the age, sex, educational and training level and capacities of the participants.

. . . .

Employment policy and human resources development

Texts adopted by the World Employment Conference

Declaration of Principles and Programme of Action adopted by the Tripartite World Conference on Employment, Income Distribution and Social Progress and the International Division of Labour (Geneva, 1976)

. . . .

PROGRAMME OF ACTION

I. BASIC NEEDS

1. Strategies and national development plans and policies should include explicitly as a priority objective the promotion of employment and the satisfaction of the basic needs of each country's population.

2. Basic needs, as understood in this Programme of Action, include two elements. First, they include certain minimum requirements of a family for private consumption: adequate food, shelter and clothing, as well as certain household equipment and furniture. Second, they include essential services provided by and for the community at large, such as safe drinking water, sanitation, public transport and health, educational and cultural facilities.

3. A basic-needs-oriented policy implies the participation of the people in making the decisions which affect them through organisations of their own choice.

4. In all countries freely chosen employment enters into a basic-needs policy both as a means and as an end. Employment yields an output. It provides an income to the employed, and gives the individual a feeling of self-respect, dignity and of being a worthy member of society.

5. It is important to recognise that the concept of basic needs is a country-specific and dynamic concept. The concept of basic needs should be placed within a context of a nation's over-all economic and social development. In no circumstances should it be taken to mean merely the minimum necessary for subsistence; it should be placed within a context of national independence, the dignity of individuals and peoples and their freedom to chart their destiny without hindrance.

. . . .

Employment Policy

9. The following policies should be adopted to encourage employment creation:

. . . .

(e) Equality of treatment and remuneration for women should be ensured.

. . . .

Standards and policy statements of special interest to women workers

Social Policies

14. Social policies should be designed to increase the welfare of working people, especially women, the young and the aged.

Women

15. Since women constitute the group on the bottom of the ladder in many developing countries in respect of employment, poverty, education, training and status, the Conference recommends that special emphasis be placed in developing countries on promoting the status, education, development and employment of women and on integrating women into the economic and civic life of the country.

16. Specifically, the Conference recommends:

(a) the abolition of every kind of discrimination as regards the right to work, pay, employment, vocational guidance and training (including in-service training), promotion in employment and access to skilled jobs;

(b) that more favourable working conditions be ensured so that women may perform their other functions in society and married women may be able to return to either full-time or part-time productive employment;

(c) that the work burden and drudgery of women be relieved by improving their working and living conditions and by providing more resources for investment in favour of women in rural areas.

. . . .

Education

20. Education is itself a basic need, and equality of access to educational services, particularly in rural areas, is therefore an important ingredient of a basic-needs strategy. Lack of access to education denies many people, and particularly women, the opportunity to participate fully and meaningfully in the social, economic, cultural and political life of the community.

21. Educational and vocational training systems should be adapted to national development needs and should avoid an élitist bias; priority should be given to adult and primary education, especially in the rural areas.

Population Policy

22. High birth rates in poverty-stricken areas are not the cause of underdevelopment but a result of it. They may, however, jeopardise the satisfaction of basic needs. It is only through the fulfilment of these needs, with special emphasis on the development of the position and status of women, that couples will be in a better position to determine the size of their family in a manner compatible with the aims of their society. The Conference is of the view that population policies consistent with the culture and the societies involved, as recommended by the 1974 World Population Conference,

should be strongly encouraged. It recommends that information on population programmes should be made available to people in a form and language that they can understand.

IV. ACTIVE MANPOWER POLICIES AND ADJUSTMENT ASSISTANCE IN DEVELOPED COUNTRIES

. . . .

Policy Measures

67. The priorities of national employment policies should be:

. . . .

(iii) the reinforcement of measures designed to provide protection against undesirable effects of cyclical evolution or structural change, such as those mentioned in ILO Conventions and Recommendations. These measures could include:

. . . .

– provision of special measures for women, migrants, young workers, and handicapped workers whose re-employment involves special problems.

These matters should be dealt with in close co-operation between governments, employers and workers.

. . . .

Texts adopted by ILO Regional Conferences

Resolution concerning Employment Service Organistion adopted by the Asian Regional Conference (Nuwara Eliya (Ceylon), 1950)

. . . .

10. The benefits of the employment service should be made available on the basis of absolute equality to all workers residing in a country without regard to nationality, sex, caste or creed.

. . . .

Conclusions concerning the Asian Manpower Plan, adopted by the Seventh Asian Regional Conference (Teheran, 1971)

. . . .

6. The reorientation of their development strategies so as to take account of employment objectives is likely to require in many Asian countries important structural reforms and shifts of emphasis in current development policies. In particular, Asian countries should–

. . . .

(b) give appropriate attention to the special problems involved in the advancement of the status of women in economic life and their effective integration in the development process;

. . . .

Standards and policy statements of special interest to women workers

HUMAN RESOURCES DEVELOPMENT

Texts adopted by the International Labour Conference

(1) Social Policy (Basic Aims and Standards) Convention, 1962 (No. 117)

. . . .

PART VI. EDUCATION AND TRAINING

Article 15

1. Adequate provision shall be made to the maximum extent possible under local conditions, for the progressive development of broad systems of education, vocational training and apprenticeship, with a view to the effective preparation of children and young persons of both sexes for a useful occupation.

2. National laws or regulations shall prescribe the school-leaving age and the minimum age for and conditions of employment.

3. In order that the child population may be able to profit by existing facilities for education and in order that the extension of such facilities may not be hindered by a demand for child labour, the employment of persons below the school-leaving age during the hours when the schools are in session shall be prohibited in areas where educational facilities are provided on a scale adequate for the majority of the children of school age.

Article 16

1. In order to secure high productivity through the development of skilled labour, training in new techniques of production shall be provided in suitable cases.

2. Such training shall be organised by or under the supervision of the competent authorities, in consultation with the employers' and workers' organisations of the country from which the trainees come and of the country of training.

. . . .

(1) Paid Educational Leave Convention, 1974 (No. 140)

. . . .

Article 8[2]

Paid educational leave shall not be denied to workers on the grounds of race, colour, sex, religion, political opinion, national extraction or social origin.

. . . .

Employment policy and human resources development

(1) Human Resources Development Convention, 1975 (No. 142)

. . . .

Article 1[3]

1. Each Member shall adopt and develop comprehensive and co-ordinated policies and programmes of vocational guidance and vocational training, closely linked with employment, in particular through public employment services.

. . . .

5. The policies and programmes shall encourage and enable all persons, on an equal basis and without any discrimination whatsoever, to develop and use their capabilities for work in their own best interests and in accordance with their own aspirations, account being taken of the needs of society.

. . . .

(1) Human Resources Development Recommendation, 1975 (No. 150)

. . . .

VIII. PROMOTION OF EQUALITY OF OPPORTUNITY OF WOMEN AND MEN IN TRAINING AND EMPLOYMENT

54. (1) Measures should be taken to promote equality of opportunity of women and men in employment and in society as a whole.

(2) These measures should form an integral part of all economic, social and cultural measures taken by governments for improving the employment situation of women and should include, as far as possible–

(a) educating the general public and in particular parents, teachers, vocational guidance and vocational training staff, the staff of employment and other social services, employers and workers, on the need for encouraging women and men to play an equal part in society and in the economy and for changing traditional attitudes regarding the work of women and men in the home and in working life;

(b) providing girls and women with vocational guidance on the same broad range of educational, vocational training and employment opportunities as boys and men, encouraging them to take full advantage of such opportunities and creating the conditions required for them to do so;

(c) promoting equality of access for girls and women to all streams of education and to vocational training for all types of occupations, including those which have been traditionally accessible only to boys and men, subject to the provisions of international labour Conventions and Recommendations;

Standards and policy statements of special interest to women workers

   (d) promoting further training for girls and women to ensure their personal development and advancement to skilled employment and posts of responsibility, and urging employers to provide them with the same opportunities of extending their work experience as offered to male workers with the same education and qualifications;
   (e) providing day-care facilities and other services for children of different ages, in so far as possible, so that girls and women with family responsibilities have access to normal vocational training, as well as making special arrangements, for instance in the form of part-time or correspondence courses, vocational training programmes following a recurrent pattern or programmes using mass media;
   (f) providing vocational training programmes for women above the normal age of entry into employment who wish to take up work for the first time or re-enter it after a period of absence.

   55. Special vocational training arrangements and programmes, similar to those envisaged in clauses (e) and (f) of subparagraph (2) of Paragraph 54 of this Recommendation, should be available to men having analogous problems.

   56. Account should be taken of the Employment Policy Convention and Recommendation, 1964, in the implementation of measures for the promotion of equality of opportunity of women and men in training and employment.

. . . .

Resolution concerning Youth Employment, adopted by the International Labour Conference at its 64th Session (Geneva, 1978)

   The General Conference of the International Labour Organisation,

. . . .

   1. Calls upon member States to devote priority attention to the elaboration of specific and effective measures against youth unemployment to be implemented in the framework of over-all full employment plans, or policies, or both, and in this context–

. . . .

   (c) to introduce, where this has not already been done, methods of education and training which combine practical work with theoretical studies, integrate vocational training into employment promotion measures and promote the skills, abilities and opportunities of individuals in employment, regardless of sex;

. . . .

   (f) to respect the principle of equal pay for equal work also in the case of young workers in order to avoid their exploitation as a source of cheap labour and duly to protect apprentices in this connection.

Employment policy and human resources development

Texts adopted by ILO Regional Conferences

Recommendations on Human Resources Development in Rural Areas in Asia and the Role of Rural Institutions, adopted by the Eighth Asian Regional Conference (Colombo, 1975)

. . . .

EDUCATION AND TRAINING

. . . .

3. To promote self-employment and salaried employment in the rural informal sector, the ILO should strengthen its technical co-operation activities in the Asian region for the non-formal vocational training of men, women and young adults in such categories as marginal and submarginal farmers, tenants, landless workers and plantation, forestry and farm workers, craftsmen, small businessmen, fishermen and other categories of rural people.

. . . .

5. In order to implement the transfer of technologies at the level of the villages, multipurpose training centres could be created, the aim of which would be to improve and develop new techniques in rural occupations for farmers, artisans, rural women and youth. ILO assistance could include in particular the planning of a network of centres, the training of instructors, defining programmes, elaborating methods and evaluating the results. There could be:

. . . .

(f) special programmes for rural women, wherever necessary, either as separate programmes or as part of the multi-purpose training centres.

. . . .

Conclusions Adopted on the Recommendation of the Committee on Education for Development by the Fifth African Regional Conference (Abidjan, 1977)

. . . .

V. PRIORITIES FOR ENABLING EDUCATION AND TRAINING IN AFRICA

. . . .

Training of Vulnerable Groups

32. Young people, women and the handicapped are the most vulnerable groups in the African context. While there is lack of skills in certain occupational categories, such as technicians and middle-level supervisors, there is a serious problem of unemployment and underemployment among

Standards and policy statements of special interest to women workers

the youth and women of African States. Efforts to reduce these imbalances can only be achieved through vigorous education and training programmes.

. . . .

36. Special efforts should be made to help women in rural areas to have access to training opportunities and consequently to income-generating employment.

37. Such efforts should not only concentrate on improving training in occupations which are predominantly women's occupations but also to provide and increase the opportunities for training in occupations which have so far not been considered as typically women's occupations.

38. Such efforts should also include the provision of training opportunities for women in occupations which require higher levels of skill and responsibilities, including managerial responsibilities.

39. Measures should be taken to extend training opportunities to women in the low-income brackets in rural and urban areas and those who are the sole breadwinners of their families. Such measures should also facilitate, through training, the re-entry of women into the employment market when social or economic reasons require them to do so.

Texts adopted by ILO Industrial Meetings, etc.

Conclusions (No. 72) concerning Training at Different Levels in the Metal Trades with Particular Reference to Developing Countries, adopted by the Metal Trades Committee at its Ninth Session (Geneva, 1971)

. . . .

EQUALITY OF ACCESS TO TRAINING

25. Within the framework of manpower requirements equality of access to training should be ensured by governments, employers and trade unions. In this connection appropriate measures should be taken to provide equal opportunity for women workers.

. . . .

Conclusions (No. 71) concerning Training Requirements in the Textiles Industry in the Light of Changes in the Occupational Structure, adopted by the Textiles Committee at its Tenth Session (Geneva, 1978)

. . . .

Training Objectives

7. Training should, at all levels, aim at developing the capacity of the individual as a whole, not just at imparting a minimum of skills and know-

ledge needed for doing the job properly. It may be necessary, however, in countries in which job training is still given with primitive methods or giving unsatisfactory results to begin by developing adequate standards and methods of skill training. This will make it possible to expand and improve training systems and programmes to include such elements of training as are necessary for providing adequate technological understanding, initiation of new workers into the industrial environment and the social patterns of life in industry and such general and technical education as will be required for promotion and personal development.

8. It is particularly important for undertakings in the textile industry employing women to arrange the recruitment and training of girls and women in such a manner that they have equal opportunities with boys and men as regards qualifications acquired, earnings and promotion.

9. Training plans and programmes should be developed on the basis of principles of continuing education and training and with a view to offering the broadest possible opportunities for employment and career.

. . . .

Resolution (No. 49) concerning Problems of Women Non-Manual Workers, adopted by the Advisory Committee on Salaried Employees and Professional Workers at its 5th Session (Cologne, 1959)

. . . .

Employment

1. Forecast studies relating to manpower needs should be developed. These studies should cover in particular the occupations and duties already open to women non-manual workers, the new careers which are being opened to them, and the qualifications and capacities required in the various jobs.

. . . .

Vocational Guidance

3. The communication of full information regarding employment to girls and to families, schools and others who influence them is of course of vital importance.

. . . .

5. The vocational guidance authorities should make a special effort to assist women seeking employment in solving problems relating to occupational choice, due account being taken of their capacities and of potential employment possibilities in various occupations and particularly in those where there is a prospect of new openings to women non-manual workers.

Standards and policy statements of special interest to women workers

Vocational Training

6. The attention of families, teachers, and the public authorities should be drawn to the fact that girls and boys should enjoy equal opportunities with regard to vocational training.

. . . .

8. Appropriate methods with regard to programmes and equipment should be developed in order to ensure the technical training of future women non-manual workers; this technical training should be comprehensive in order to permit adaptation, in the course of employment, to the new conditions resulting from the introduction of new techniques.

9. When new techniques of work are introduced in an undertaking, the employer should ensure the adaptation or vocational training of women non-manual employees during working hours.

10. Any further training facilities provided by employers to non-manual workers should be made available without discrimination on grounds of sex.

Occupational Re-adaptation

11. The public authorities, working in co-operation with employers' and workers' organisations, should establish procedures for the re-adaptation of women non-manual workers who have lost their jobs as a result of the introduction of new techniques, or who have been out of the labour force for many years.

. . . .

Conclusions (No. 12) concerning Appropriate Technology for Employment Creation in the Food-Processing and Drink Industries of Developing Countries, adopted by the Second Tripartite Technical Meeting for the Food Products and Drink Industries (Geneva, 1978)

. . . .

17. The role of women in the industrialisation process is mentioned both in the Declaration adopted by the ILO's World Employment Conference in 1976, and in the Lima Declaration adopted by the Second General Conference of UNIDO in 1975. Both declarations noted the need for women to have equal rights. Furthermore, and specifically in relation to the food industries, more training facilities should be provided for women workers, and professional scientists and technologists. Moreover, additional research and development should be carried out to upgrade traditional small-scale and village-level technologies, presently used mainly by women in many developing countries, so as to improve their working conditions, and reduce drudgery.

. . . .

Employment policy and human resources development

Conclusions (No. 1) concerning the Effects of Technological Developments on the Occupational Structure of Employment in the Leather and Footwear Industry, adopted by the Tripartite Technical Meeting for the Leather and Footwear Industry (Geneva, 1969)

. . . .

Effects on the Composition of Employment

9. Technological developments will reduce the over-all number of jobs. This reduction will particularly affect skilled workers. However, technological developments will increase needs, both in number and quality, for more highly skilled workers such as technicians, chemists, designers, maintenance personnel, etc. The role of middle management will become more important and will require a higher level of technical proficiency as well as the ability to maintain good human relationships with the workers. Technological developments are likely to accelerate the trend towards the employment of a greater proportion of women workers. These various trends have implications for vocational training policies.

SUGGESTIONS FOR ACTION BY THE INDUSTRY AND BY GOVERNMENTS

. . . .

11. In the field of vocational training, attention must be given to much more broadly based initial training including some theoretical instruction in the whole manufacturing process in the industry. Training should be continuous and should allow for smooth retraining for the new needs of the industry. Training should open up avenues of advancement to employment in technical occupations in the industry and in middle management. In those countries where women constitute a high proportion of the labour force, more attention than hitherto should be given to their training.

. . . .

Notes

[1] Similar provisions are also contained in Paragraph 1 of the Employment Policy Recommendation, 1964 (No. 122), below.

[2] A similar provision is contained in Paragraph 13 of the Paid Educational Leave Recommendation, 1974 (No. 148).

[3] Similar provisions are contained in Paragraph 4 of the Human Resources Development Recommendation, 1975 (No. 150), below.

CONDITIONS OF WORK AND SOCIAL POLICY 3

NIGHT WORK

Text adopted by the International Labour Conference

(1 and 2) Night Work (Women) Convention (Revised), 1948 (No. 89)[1]

. . . .

Article 3

Women without distinction of age shall not be employed during the night in any public or private industrial undertaking, or in any branch thereof, other than an undertaking in which only members of the same family are employed.

Article 4

Article 3 shall not apply–

(a) in cases of *force majeure*, when in any undertaking there occurs an interruption of work which it was impossible to foresee, and which is not of a recurring character;
(b) in cases where the work has to do with raw materials or materials in course of treatment which are subject to rapid deterioration when such night work is necessary to preserve the said materials from certain loss.

Article 5

1. The prohibition of night work for women may be suspended by the government, after consultation with the employers' and workers' organisations concerned, when in case of serious emergency the national interest demands it.

2. Such suspension shall be notified by the government concerned to the Director-General of the International Labour Office in its annual report on the application of the Convention.

Standards and policy statements of special interest to women workers

Article 6

In industrial undertakings which are influenced by the seasons and in all cases where exceptional circumstances demand it, the night period may be reduced to ten hours on sixty days of the year.

Article 7

In countries where the climate renders work by day particularly trying, the night period may be shorter than that prescribed in the above articles if compensatory rest is accorded during the day.

Article 8

This Convention does not apply to—

(a) women holding responsible positions of a managerial or technical character; and

(b) women employed in health and welfare services who are not ordinarily engaged in manual work.

PART II. SPECIAL PROVISIONS FOR CERTAIN COUNTRIES

Article 9

In those countries where no government regulation as yet applies to the employment of women in industrial undertakings during the night, the term "night" may provisionally, and for a maximum period of three years, be declared by the government to signify a period of only ten hours, including an interval prescribed by the competent authority of at least seven consecutive hours falling between ten o'clock in the evening and seven o'clock in the morning.

. . . .

Texts adopted by ILO Industrial Meetings, etc.

Conclusions (No. 72) concerning Conditions of Work in the Textiles Industry including Problems Related to Organisation of Work, adopted by the Textiles Committee at its Tenth Session (Geneva, 1978)

. . . .

8. Night work by women in the textile industry should be adequately regulated, taking into account their role in the family and in society. In so doing, it should be possible to take into account the relevant ILO standards on this subject, whose revision is being envisaged.

. . . .

Conditions of work and social policy

12. Workers on shifts, especially on night shifts, should have access to adequate social services (hot food, rest-rooms, crèches, kindergartens, medical services) organised either inside or outside the undertaking.

. . . .

14. The effective length of working time should not exceed limits compatible with the health and welfare of workers, especially women and young workers. Where the maximum daily working time has not been determined by collective agreements, it should be fixed by the legislation of each country. Every hour worked over and above the normal time fixed by legislation or collective agreements should be considered as overtime and remunerated at a suitably higher rate, that is to say taking into account the fatigue caused and the importance of the sacrifice imposed on the worker through reduction of his free time.

. . . .

HOURS OF WORK

Texts adopted by the International Labour Conference

(1) Reduction of Hours of Work Recommendation, 1962 (No. 116)

. . . .

9. In carrying out measures for progressively reducing hours of work, priority should be given to industries and occupations which involve a particularly heavy physical or mental strain or health risks for the workers concerned, particularly where these consist mainly of women and young persons.

. . . .

18. In arranging overtime, due consideration should be given to the special circumstances of young persons under 18 years of age, of pregnant women and nursing mothers and of handicapped persons.

. . . .

Resolution concerning Part-Time Employment, adopted by the International Labour Conference at its 48th Session (Geneva, 1964)

The General Conference of the International Labour Organisation,

Recognising the fact that part-time work does occur, particularly in countries with full employment and that it can give a partial answer to individual social needs of men and women,

Considering that governments and employers' and workers' organisations should pay attention to it and should find all the necessary safeguards in the framework of social legislation and collective agreements,

Recognising that part-time work can be of particular interest for women with family responsibilities who wish to do so,

Noting that the nature of certain kinds of work can meet these requirements,

Recognising that part-time work presents certain problems,

Noting that there is not sufficient information and knowledge in this field;

Invites the International Labour Office–

(1) to give a precise definition of what is meant by "part-time work";

(2) to undertake, in co-operation with the competent authorities and the organisations of employers and workers, inquiries to determine–

(a) the number and nature of part-time employment opportunities; and

(b) the number and characteristics of persons who have or seek part-time employment.

Texts adopted by ILO Industrial Meetings, etc.

Conclusions (No. 57) concerning the Impact of Social and Economic Developments on Working and Living Conditions in the Distributive Trades, adopted by the Advisory Committee on Salaried Employees and Professional Workers at its 6th Session (Geneva, 1967)

. . . .

Hours of Work

54. It is noted that there is a trend toward the progressive reduction of normal working hours, which might contribute to ensuring employment of the greatest possible number of workers.

55. This trend also ensures the participation of the workers, with regard to a fundamental aspect of working and living conditions, in general economic and social progress.

56. Wherever there is a trend towards reducing normal working hours, distributive workers should benefit from such measures as do workers in other sectors of economic activity.

57. In this connection, particular attention should be given, on the one hand, to the high proportion of women workers and of young workers in the distributive trades, and on the other, to the fact that in many of the occupations concerned there is increasing strain and stress resulting from the working and environmental conditions.

58. Exceptions from the normal daily and weekly working hours and other derogations should be gradually reduced whenever possible.

. . . .

Conclusions (No. 71) concerning Conditions of Work and Life of Employees in Commerce and Offices, adopted by the Advisory Committee on Salaried Employees and Professional Workers at its Seventh Session (Geneva, 1974)

. . . .

Flexible Working Hours

21. Flexible working hours meet the needs of workers, and in particular workers with family responsibilities.

22. However, they cannot provide a satisfactory answer to the needs of employees unless they are organised in an appropriate way. Provisions concerning flexible working hours should be worked out with the participation of workers and/or their representatives. Their application should be carried out through consultation with them in order to safeguard the interests of the employees concerned.

. . . .

Temporary Work

27. Employees may wish to work on a temporary basis for personal reasons, and particularly for family reasons, while employers may require temporary manpower for reasons of greater flexibility.

28. The fact that salaried employees are working on a temporary basis should not deprive them of the rights and advantages accorded to other workers–written contract, normal hours of work, weekly rest, annual leave, sick leave, remuneration, social security and other social benefits–and appropriate regulations should be drawn up or adapted to guarantee them adequate protection in this respect.

29. All temporary employees should be able to obtain permanent employment so long as they meet the necessary requirements when such employment is available.

. . . .

Conclusions (No. 2) concerning Conditions of Employment and Related Problems in the Leather and Footwear Industry, with Particular Reference to Countries in the course of Industrialisation, adopted by the Tripartite Meeting for the Leather and Footwear Industry (Geneva, 1969)

. . . .

HOURS OF WORK

. . . .

13. Actual hours of work should not exceed the limits compatible with the health and well-being of the workers, particularly women and young workers.

14. In order to ensure adequate earnings and the security of a regular income for the workers, it seems necessary to take measures to regularise hours of work, production and employment throughout the year. If this is not possible, legislation or negotiation could alleviate hardship by the provision of unemployment benefits or similar benefits.

. . . .

OCCUPATIONAL SAFETY, HEALTH AND WELFARE

Texts adopted by the International Labour Conference

(1) White Lead (Painting) Convention, 1921 (No. 13)

. . . .

Article 3

1. The employment of males under eighteen years of age and of all females shall be prohibited in any painting work of an industrial character involving the use of white lead or sulphate of lead or other products containing these pigments.

. . . .

(1) Underground Work (Women) Convention, 1935 (No. 45)

. . . .

Article 2

No female, whatever her age, shall be employed on underground work in any mine.

Article 3

National laws or regulations may exempt from the above prohibition—

(a) females holding positions of management who do not perform manual work;

(b) females employed in health and welfare services;

(c) females who, in the course of their studies, spend a period of training in the underground parts of a mine; and

(d) any other females who may occasionally have to enter the underground parts of a mine for the purpose of a non-manual occupation.

. . . .

Conditions of work and social policy

(1) Maximum Weight Convention, 1967 (No. 127)

. . . .

Article 7

1. The assignment of women and young workers to manual transport of loads other than light loads shall be limited.

2. Where women and young workers are engaged in the manual transport of loads, the maximum weight of such loads shall be substantially less than that permitted for adult male workers.

. . . .

(1) Maximum Weight Recommendation, 1967 (No. 128)

. . . .

B. WOMEN WORKERS

15. Where adult women workers are engaged in the manual transport of loads, the maximum weight of such loads should be substantially less than that permitted for adult male workers.

16. As far as possible, adult women workers should not be assigned to regular manual transport of loads.

17. Where adult women workers are assigned to regular manual transport of loads, provision should be made–

(a) as appropriate, to reduce the time spent on actual lifting, carrying and putting down of loads by such workers;

(b) to prohibit the assignment of such workers to certain specified jobs, comprised in manual transport of loads, which are especially arduous.

18. No woman should be assigned to manual transport of loads during a pregnancy which has been medically determined or during the ten weeks following confinement if in the opinion of a qualified physician such work is likely to impair her health or that of her child.

. . . .

(1) Benzene Convention, 1971 (No. 136)

. . . .

Article 11[1]

1. Women medically certified as pregnant, and nursing mothers, shall not be employed in work processes involving exposure to benzene or products containing benzene.

. . . .

Standards and policy statements of special interest to women workers

(1) Welfare Facilities Recommendation, 1956 (No. 102)

. . . .

16. (1) In undertakings where any workers, especially women and young workers, have in the course of their work reasonable opportunities for sitting without detriment to their work, seats should be provided and maintained for their use.

(2) Seats so provided should be in adequate numbers and reasonably near the work posts of the workers concerned.

. . . .

19. (1) In an undertaking where alternative facilities are not available for workers to take temporary rest during working hours, a rest room should be provided, where this is desirable, having regard to the nature of the work and any other relevant conditions and circumstances. In particular, rest rooms should be provided to meet the needs of women workers; of workers engaged on particularly arduous or special work requiring temporary rest during working hours; or of workers employed on broken shifts.

. . . .

(1 and 2) Occupational Health Services Recommendation, 1959 (No. 112)

. . . .

8. The functions of occupational health services should be progressively developed, in accordance with the circumstances and having regard to the extent to which one or more of these functions are adequately discharged in accordance with national law or practice by other appropriate services, so that they will include in particular the following:

. . . .

(e) pre-employment, periodic and special medical examinations–including, where necessary, biological and radiological examinations–prescribed by national laws or regulations, or by agreements between the parties or organisations concerned, or considered advisable for preventive purposes by the industrial physician; such examinations should ensure particular surveillance over certain classes of workers, such as women, young persons, workers exposed to special risks and handicapped persons;

. . . .

(1 and 2) Radiation Protection Recommendation, 1960 (No. 114)

. . . .

16. In view of the special medical problems involved in the employment of women of child-bearing age in radiation work every care should be taken to ensure that they are not exposed to high radiation risks.

. . . .

Declaration on Equality of Opportunity and Treatment for Women Workers, adopted by the International Labour Conference at its 60th Session (Geneva, 1975)

. . . .

Article 9

(1) Protection of women at work shall be an integral part of the efforts aimed at continuous promotion and improvement of living and working conditions of all employees.

(2) Women shall be protected from risks inherent in their employment and occupation on the same basis and with the same standards of protection as men, in the light of advances in scientific and technological knowledge.

(3) Studies and research shall be undertaken into processes which might have a harmful effect on women and men from the standpoint of their social function of reproduction.

(4) Measures shall be taken to extend special protection to women for types of work proved to be harmful for them from the standpoint of their social function of reproduction and such measures shall be reviewed and brought up-to-date periodically in the light of advances in scientific and technological knowledge.

. . . .

Resolution concerning a Plan of Action with a view to promoting Equality of Opportunity and Treatment for Women Workers, adopted by the International Labour Conference at its 60th Session (Geneva, 1975)

. . . .

6. Review of Protective Legislation

Measures should be taken to review all protective legislation applying to women in the light of up-to-date scientific knowledge and technological advances and to revise, supplement, extend to all workers, retain, or repeal such legislation according to national circumstances, these measures being aimed at the improvement of the quality of life.

. . . .

Texts adopted by ILO Regional Conferences

Resolution concerning the Employment of Women and the Protection of Maternity, adopted by the Preparatory Asian Regional Conference (New Delhi, 1947)

. . . .

Standards and policy statements of special interest to women workers

B. PROTECTION OF WOMEN ENGAGED IN HEAVY LABOUR

8. Protection from arduous conditions of work should be provided for women workers in occupations involving heavy labour who in some countries or occupations are excluded from protection of the existent laws in respect of hours of work, conditions of work, social security and holidays with pay, etc. and this protection should extend to those women who work as helpers or are recruited under a contract system of employment in these occupations.

9. Protection from serious risks to the health of women engaged in these occupations should be provided progressively with special regard for the following considerations:

(a) weights to be lifted, carried or loaded or unloaded should be limited by national laws or regulations with due regard to the physique of the worker, the method employed in lifting or carrying, the instruction in such methods to be supplied to the worker, the distances and heights involved and the frequency of lifting or carrying required, in accordance with scientifically established standards;

(b) employers should be required to provide separate and suitable accommodation in workplaces to serve as wash rooms, toilets, dressing rooms, etc., for women;

(c) in the interests of the health and comfort of women workers, employers should be required to provide them with, wherever feasible, a sufficient number of seats at places of work and rest.

10. The foregoing measures of protection should be extended to women in large-scale agriculture or plantations as soon as means and facilities for the enforcement of these measures are available.

. . . .

Resolution concerning the Promotion of Facilities for Workers' Welfare in Asian Countries, adopted by the Asian Regional Conference (Nuwara Eliya (Ceylon), 1950)

. . . .

The Conference calls the attention of the Asian countries to the following principles, which seem to provide a suitable basis for the promotion of facilities for workers' welfare in Asian countries:

1. (1) The basic requirements in respect of workers' welfare facilities, such as occupational health facilities and reasonable medical and maternity facilities, canteens and other feeding arrangements and child care services, should be prescribed by legislation defining–

(a) the minimum standards to be observed, in particular as regards construction, equipment and personnel; and *(b)* the scope of application, which should include the largest possible number of undertakings, whether public or private, and of workers and should be widened progressively.

. . . .

Resolution concerning Conditions of Work and Life, adopted by the Ninth Conference of American States Members (Caracas, 1970)

The Ninth Conference of American States Members of the International Labour Organisation,

. . . .

Recognising that in certain cases, and in some countries, various social services are provided for workers at the enterprise and trade union level, which make an important contribution to improving their living and working conditions,

Considering, however, that such services are at present available only to limited numbers of workers;

1. Urges countries of the American region to prepare and carry out a realistic policy to improve conditions of work and life which should–

(a) provide social protection to all workers without distinction, and particularly to groups which may need special protection, such as women workers, domestic workers, migrant workers, rural workers and unemployed and incapacitated workers, as well as to indigenous populations;

(b) correspond to actual needs and to the practical possibilities of meeting those needs;

(c) contribute to economic and social development by stimulating the growth of employment and productivity, by protecting the health and welfare of workers and by ensuring that workers enjoy their fair share of the fruits of increases in productivity.

. . . .

Texts adopted by ILO Industrial Meetings, etc.

Memorandum (No. 31) concerning Women's Employment in the Textiles Industry, adopted by the Textiles Committee at its 4th Session (Geneva, 1953)

. . . .

WELFARE SERVICES

4. The Committee recognises that in many countries efforts have been made to provide suitable welfare services for women workers and that they have had considerable success in this respect.

Standards and policy statements of special interest to women workers

5. Where the textile industry employs large numbers of women with home responsibilities, welfare services should be established and, where required, improved to safeguard the interests and needs of these women and their children.

6. In order to safeguard the health and welfare of women workers, and to promote their efficiency at work, it is desirable to provide, by legislation or collective agreements or other appropriate means—

(a) maternity protection, particularly in respect of maternity leave, maternity benefits, facilities for nursing mothers and infants, protection of employment and protection of the health of working women during the maternity period, in which connection attention is called to the principles contained in the Maternity Protection Convention and Recommendation, 1952;

(b) adequate protection against employment on heavy or other work which may be prejudicial to health;

(c) welfare facilities in the factory such as appropriate seating accommodation (the need for which should be brought to the attention of textile machine manufacturers), rest rooms and sanitary provisions;

(d) abolition of night work for women workers.

7. It would also be desirable, wherever after joint consultation between employers and workers it had been found necessary and practicable, to establish and develop, by legislation or collective agreements or other appropriate means, social services such as—

(a) canteens and suitable transport facilities, as well as crèches or day nurseries which should conform to appropriate standards and preferably should be located outside the factory;

(b) where these may be organised under the appropriate competent authority or by other means, services such as school meals and home helps in order to lighten the household duties of working women;

. . . .

(d) women welfare officers to deal with the special problems of women workers.

8. The financing of certain welfare and social services provided particularly for women workers or their children should, wherever appropriate, be wholly or partly a charge upon the community and should not be borne by the employer to such an extent as to jeopardise the employment opportunities of women in the textile industry.

. . . .

Conclusions (No. 72) concerning Conditions of Work in the Textiles Industry, including Problems Related to Organisation of Work, adopted at the Tenth Session of the Textiles Committee (Geneva, 1978)

. . . .

3. The competent authorities should formulate, in consultation with employers' and workers' representatives, appropriate legislation assuring the protection of minimum working conditions for all workers, including textile workers. This legislation should include provisions protecting working conditions for women and young workers.

4. Where other appropriate arrangements have not been made, the competent authorities must organise adequate inspection services to control systematically the application of legislation on working conditions and appropriate sanctions should be applied in the case of non-observation of this legislation.

. . . .

FACILITIES AND SERVICES FOR WOMEN WORKERS WITH FAMILY RESPONSIBILITIES

Texts adopted by the International Labour Conference

(3) Employment (Women with Family Responsibilities) Recommendation, 1965 (No. 123)[3]

. . . .

Noting the fact that in many countries women are working outside their homes in increasing numbers as an integral and essential part of the labour force, and

Noting further that many such women have special problems arising out of the need to reconcile their dual family and work responsibilities, and

Noting that many of these problems, though they have particular relevance to the opportunities for employment of women workers with family responsibilities, also confront other workers and can be substantially alleviated by measures affecting all workers, such as the progressive reduction of daily and weekly hours of work, and

Noting further that many of the special problems faced by women with family responsibilities are not problems peculiar to women workers but are problems of the family and of society as a whole, and

Recognising that continuous social adaptation is required to meet these problems in a manner consistent with the best interests of all concerned, and

Aware of the need for governments and for all public and private organisations concerned to give consideration to these problems in a broad social, economic and legal context,

. . . .

The Conference recommends that each Member should apply the following provisions as fully and as rapidly as national conditions allow:

Standards and policy statements of special interest to women workers

I. General Principle

1. The competent authorities should, in co-operation with the public and private organisations concerned, in particular employers' and workers' organisations, and in accordance with national and local needs and possibilities–

(a) pursue an appropriate policy with a view to enabling women with family responsibilities who work outside their homes to exercise their right to do so without being subject to discrimination and in accordance with the principles laid down in the Discrimination (Employment and Occupation) Convention, 1958, as well as in other standards relating to women adopted by the International Labour Conference; and

(b) encourage, facilitate or themselves undertake the development of services to enable women to fulfil their various responsibilities at home and at work harmoniously.

II. Public Information and Education

2. The competent authorities should, in co-operation with the public and private organisations concerned, in particular employers' and workers' organisations, take appropriate steps–

(a) to encourage such consideration of the problems of women workers with family responsibilities as may be necessary to help these workers to become effectively integrated in the labour force on the basis of equal rights;

(b) to undertake or promote such research as may be necessary and feasible into the various aspects of the employment of women workers with family responsibilities with a view to presenting objective information on which sound policies and measures may be based; and

(c) to engender broader public understanding of the problems of these workers with a view to developing community policies and a climate of opinion conducive to helping them to meet their family and employment responsibilities.

III. Child-Care Services and Facilities

3. With a view to determining the scope and character of the child-care services and facilities needed to assist women workers to meet their employment and family responsibilities, the competent authorities should, in co-operation with the public and private organisations concerned, in particular employers' and workers' organisations, and within the scope of their resources for collecting information, take such measures as may be necessary and appropriate–

(a) to collect and publish adequate statistics on the number of mothers engaged in or seeking employment and on the number and age of their children; and

Conditions of work and social policy

(b) to ascertain, through systematic surveys conducted more particularly in local communities, the needs and preferences for child-care arrangements organised outside the family.

4. The competent authorities should, in co-operation with the public and private organisations concerned, take appropriate steps to ensure that child-care services and facilities meet the needs and preferences so revealed; to this end they should, taking account of national and local circumstances and possibilities, in particular–

(a) encourage and facilitate the establishment, particularly in local communities, of plans for the systematic development of child-care services and facilities; and

(b) themselves organise as well as encourage and facilitate the provision of adequate and appropriate child-care services and facilities, at reasonable charge or free in case of need, developed along flexible lines and meeting the needs of children of different ages and of their working parents.

5. With a view to safeguarding the health and welfare of the child–

(a) child-care services and facilities of all types should comply with standards laid down and supervised by the competent authorities;

(b) such standards should prescribe in particular the equipment and hygienic requirements of the services and facilities provided and the number and qualifications of the staff; and

(c) the competent authorities should provide or help to ensure the provision of adequate training at various levels for the personnel needed to staff child-care services and facilities.

6. The competent authorities should, with the co-operation and participation of the public and private organisations concerned, in particular employers' and workers' organisations, help to ensure public understanding and support for efforts made to meet the special needs of working parents in respect of child-care services and facilities.

IV. Entry and Re-entry into Employment

7. The competent authorities should take all measures in accordance with the Employment Policy Convention, 1964, and the Employment Policy Recommendation, 1964, to enable women with family responsibilities to become or to remain integrated in the labour force as well as to re-enter the labour force.

8. With a view to enabling women with family reponsibilities to become integrated in the labour force on a footing of equality, and with a view to facilitating their entry into employment or their re-entry after a comparatively long period of absence, the competent authorities should, in co-operation with the public and private organisations concerned, in particular employers' and workers' organisations, take all measures that may be necessary in the national circumstances–

(a) to ensure the provision for girls of general education, vocational guidance and vocational training free from any form of discrimination on the ground of sex;
(b) to encourage girls to obtain a sound vocational preparation as a basis for their future work lives; and
(c) to convince parents and educators of the need to give girls a sound vocational preparation.

9. (1) The competent authorities should, in co-operation with the public and private organisations concerned and taking account of national needs and possibilities, provide or help to ensure the provision of the services that may be necessary to facilitate the entry into employment of women who have not yet worked, or the re-entry into employment of women who have been out of the employment market for a comparatively long time, owing, in particular, to family responsibilities.

(2) Such services should be organised within the framework of existing services for all workers or, in default thereof, along lines appropriate to national conditions; they should include adequate counselling, information and placement services and provide adequate vocational training and retraining facilities appropriate to the needs of the women concerned and available without distinction as regards age.

(3) The services and facilities should be kept under review in order to ensure that they are properly adapted to the special needs of these women workers and to the changing needs and tendencies of economic and technological development.

10. (1) In the case of women who, on account of their family responsibilities arising out of maternity, do not find themselves in a position to return to their employment immediately following exhaustion of the normal period of maternity leave established by law or practice, appropriate measures should be taken to the extent possible to allow them a reasonable further period of leave of absence without relinquishing their employment, all rights resulting from their employment being fully safeguarded.

(2) In case of termination of employment following maternity, the women concerned should be considered for re-employment in accordance with the provisions applicable under the Termination of Employment Recommendation, 1963, to workers whose employment has been terminated owing to a reduction of the workforce.[4]

V. MISCELLANEOUS PROVISIONS

11. (1) To the extent necessary the public and private organisations concerned, in particular employers' and workers' organisations, should co-operate with the competent authorities and collaborate with each other to take other measures and promote other action to assist women workers to meet their employment and family responsibilities without detriment to their opportunities for employment and promotion.

(2) In this connection attention should be given, as local needs require and possibilities permit, to matters which have particular relevance for women workers with family responsibilities, such as the organisation of public transport, the harmonisation of working hours and hours of schools and child-care services or facilities, and the provision at low cost of the facilities required to simplify and lighten household tasks.

12. Particular efforts should be made to develop home-aid services operating under public authority or supervision and providing women workers with family responsibilities, in the event of family need, with qualified assistance at reasonable charge.

Texts adopted by ILO Industrial Meetings, etc.

Resolution (No. 81) concerning Working Mothers Employed in the Textiles Industry, adopted by the Textiles Committee at its 10th Session (Geneva, 1978)

. . . .

Considering that the protection of the rights of women, children and young persons is one of the statutory objectives of the ILO and that, in accordance with the Declaration of Philadelphia, the International Labour Organisation must contribute to the adoption by all countries of the world of programmes aimed in particular at safeguarding the welfare of children and mothers,

. . . .

Referring to the Employment (Women with Family Responsibilities) Recommendation, 1965 (No. 123), which stresses that the competent authorities should, in co-operation with workers' and employers' organisations, encourage, facilitate and undertake the development of services to enable women to fulfil their various responsibilities at home and at work harmoniously,

Bearing in mind that the employment of women, including married women, is increasing in many countries and that their role in the economy is becoming more and more important,

Emphasising that in most countries women constitute the greater part of the labour force in the textile industry,

Noting that many women employed in the textile industry face special problems arising from the combination of their family and work responsibilities,

Recognising the need to improve the situation of working mothers in textile undertakings and to adopt extensive social measures to this end,

. . . .

The Textiles Committee invites the Governing Body of the International Labour Office:

Standards and policy statements of special interest to women workers

(1) to draw the attention of the governments of the States Members of the ILO and, through them, that of the organisations of workers and employers to the need to take measures aimed at improving the situation of working mothers in the textiles industry, creating and developing a network of home-aid services, increasing the number of pre-school establishments required to assist women workers to meet their family and occupational responsibilities, and to apply measures for the purpose of facilitating and improving the work of women;

. . . .

Conclusions (No. 1) concerning the Effects of Technological Developments on the Occupational Structure of Employment in the Leather and Footwear Industry, adopted by the Tripartite Technical Meeting for the Leather and Footwear Industry (Geneva, 1969)

. . . .

13. Where women workers with family responsibilities form an increasing part of the labour force, action by the industry and by the community should be taken in accordance with the Employment (Women with Family Responsibilities) Recommendation, 1965 (No. 123), to enable them to fulfil their various responsibilities at home and at work harmoniously, and to facilitate their employment on a part-time basis.

. . . .

Conclusions (No. 2) concerning Conditions of Employment and Related Problems in the Leather and Footwear Industry, with Particular Reference to Countries in the course of Industrialisation, adopted by the Tripartite Technical Meeting for the Leather and Footwear Industry (Geneva, 1969)

. . . .

19. Because of the large number of working mothers employed in the industry, it is important for appropriate and adequate child care facilities to be provided so that such mothers can reconcile their occupational and family responsibilities without prejudice to their health, welfare and family responsibilities.

. . . .

Notes

[1] The Night Work (Women) Convention, 1919 (No. 4), and the Night Work (Women) Convention (Revised), 1939 (No. 91), ceased to be open to ratifications. However, Convention No. 41 remains in force in its actual form and content for those members which have ratified it but have not ratified the revising Convention No. 89.

[2] A similar provision is contained in Paragraph 19 of the Benzene Recommendation, 1971 (No. 144).

[3] In 1975 the Conference adopted a resolution concerning equal status and equal opportunity for women and men in occupation and employment in which the Governing Body was invited, on the basis of the reports under article 19 of the Constitution to be supplied by member States in 1977 on Recommendation No. 123, to place on the agenda of an early session of the

Conference the question of workers with family responsibilities, with a view to the adoption of a new instrument.

In March 1978 the Committee of Experts on the Application of Conventions and Recommendations carried out a general survey of the reports supplied by member States under article 19 on Recommendation No. 123 and the Governing Body, at its 208th (November 1978) Session, decided to include in the agenda of the 66th (1980) Session of the Conference, with a view to the adoption of an instrument or instruments, an item entitled "Equal opportunities and equal treatment for men and women workers: workers with family responsibilities".

[4] Paragraph 16 of the Termination of Employment Recommendation (No. 119) provides that (1) Workers whose employment has been terminated owing to a reduction of the workforce should be given priority of re-engagement, to the extent possible, by the employer when he again engages workers; (2) Such priority of re-engagement may be limited to a specified period of time where appropriate, the question of the retention of seniority rights should be determined in accordance with national laws or regulations, collective agreements or other appropriate national practices.

SOCIAL SECURITY 4

MATERNITY PROTECTION

Texts adopted by the International Labour Conference

(1 and 2) Maternity Protection Convention, 1919 (No. 3)

. . . .

Article 1

1. For the purpose of this Convention, the term "industrial undertaking" includes particularly–
(a) mines, quarries, and other works for the extraction of minerals from the earth;
(b) industries in which articles are manufactured, altered, cleaned, repaired, ornamented, finished, adapted for sale, broken up or demolished, or in which materials are transformed; including ship-building and the generation, transformation, and transmission of electricity or motive power of any kind;
(c) construction, reconstruction, maintenance, repair, alteration, or demolition of any building, railway, tramway, harbour, dock, pier, canal, inland waterway, road, tunnel, bridge, viaduct, sewer, drain, well, telegraphic or telephonic installation, electrical undertaking, gas work, water work or other work of construction, as well as the preparation for or laying the foundation of any such work or structure;
(d) transport of passengers or goods by road, rail, sea, or inland waterway, including the handling of goods at docks, quays, wharves, and warehouses, but excluding transport by hand.

2. For the purpose of this Convention, the term "commercial undertaking" includes any place where articles are sold or where commerce is carried on.

3. The competent authority in each country shall define the line of division which separates industry and commerce from agriculture.

Standards and policy statements of special interest to women workers

Article 2

For the purpose of this Convention, the term "woman" signifies any female person, irrespective of age or nationality, whether married or unmarried, and the term "child" signifies any child whether legitimate or illegitimate.

Article 3

In any public or private industrial or commercial undertaking, or in any branch thereof, other than an undertaking in which only members of the same family are employed, a woman–

(a) shall not be permitted to work during the six weeks following her confinement;
(b) shall have the right to leave her work if she produces a medical certificate stating that her confinement will probably take place within six weeks;
(c) shall, while she is absent from her work in pursuance of paragraphs *(a)* and *(b)*, be paid benefits sufficient for the full and healthy maintenance of herself and her child, provided either out of public funds or by means of a system of insurance, the exact amount of which shall be determined by the competent authority in each country, and as an additional benefit shall be entitled to free attendance by a doctor or certified midwife; no mistake of the medical adviser in estimating the date of confinement shall preclude a woman from receiving these benefits from the date of the medical certificate up to the date on which the confinement actually takes place;
(d) shall in any case, if she is nursing her child, be allowed half an hour twice a day during her working hours for this purpose.

Article 4

Where a woman is absent from her work in accordance with paragraphs *(a)* or *(b)* of Article 3 of this Convention, or remains absent from her work for a longer period as a result of illness medically certified to arise out of pregnancy or confinement and rendering her unfit for work, it shall not be lawful, until her absence shall have exceeded a maximum period to be fixed by the competent authority in each country, for her employer to give her notice of dismissal during such absence, nor to give her notice of dismissal at such a time that the notice would expire during such absence.

Article 5

The formal ratifications of this Convention, under the conditions set forth in the Constitution of the International Labour Organisation, shall be communicated to the Director-General of the International Labour Office for registration.

Social security

Article 6

1. Each Member of the International Labour Organisation which ratifies this Convention engages to apply it to its colonies, protectorates, and possessions which are not fully self-governing–

(a) except where, owing to the local conditions, its provisions are inapplicable; or

(b) subject to such modifications as may be necessary to adapt its provisions to local conditions.

2. Each Member shall notify to the International Labour Office the action taken in respect of each of its colonies, protectorates, and possessions which are not fully self-governing.

Article 7

As soon as the ratifications of two Members of the International Labour Organisation have been registered with the International Labour Office, the Director-General of the International Labour Office shall so notify all the Members of the International Labour Organisation.

Article 8

This Convention shall come into force at the date on which such notification is issued by the Director-General of the International Labour Office, but it shall then be binding only upon those Members which have registered their ratifications with the International Labour Office. Thereafter this Convention will come into force for any other Member at the date on which its ratification is registered with the International Labour Office.

Article 9

Each Member which ratifies this Convention agrees to bring its provisions into operation not later than 1 July 1922, and to take such action as may be necessary to make these provisions effective.

Article 10

A Member which has ratified this Convention may denounce it after the expiration of ten years from the date on which the Convention first comes into force, by an act communicated to the Director-General of the International Labour Office for registration. Such denunciation shall not take effect until one year after the date on which it is registered with the International Labour Office.

Article 11

At least once in ten years the Governing Body of the International Labour Office shall present to the General Conference a report on the working of this Convention, and shall consider the desirability of placing on the agenda of the Conference the question of its revision or modification.

. . . .

(1) Social Security (Minimum Standards) Convention, 1952 (No. 102)

. . . .

PART VIII. MATERNITY BENEFIT

Article 46

Each Member for which this Part of this Convention is in force shall secure to the persons protected the provision of maternity benefit in accordance with the following Articles of this Part.

Article 47

The contingencies covered shall include pregnancy and confinement and their consequences, and suspension of earnings, as defined by national laws or regulations, resulting therefrom.

Article 48

The persons protected shall comprise–

(a) all women in prescribed classes of employees, which classes constitute not less than 50 per cent of all employees and, for maternity medical benefit, also the wives of men in these classes; or

(b) all women in prescribed classes of the economically active population, which classes constitute not less than 20 per cent of all residents, and, for maternity medical benefit, also the wives of men in these classes; or

(c) where a declaration made in virtue of Article 3[1] is in force, all women in prescribed classes of employees, which classes constitute not less than 50 per cent of all employees in industrial workplaces employing 20 persons or more, and, for maternity medical benefit, also the wives of men in these classes.

Article 49

1. In respect of pregnancy and confinement and their consequences, the maternity medical benefit shall be medical care as specified in paragraphs 2 and 3 of this Article.

2. The medical care shall include at least–

(a) prenatal, confinement and postnatal care either by medical practitioners or by qualified midwives; and

Social security

(b) hospitalisation where necessary.

3. The medical care specified in paragraph 2 of this Article shall be afforded with a view to maintaining, restoring or improving the health of the woman protected and her ability to work and to attend to her personal needs.

4. The institutions or government departments administering the maternity medical benefit shall, by such means as may be deemed appropriate, encourage the women protected to avail themselves of the general health services placed at their disposal by the public authorities or by other bodies recognised by the public authorities.

Article 50

In respect of suspension of earnings resulting from pregnancy and from confinement and their consequences, the benefit shall be a periodical payment calculated in such a manner as to comply either with the requirements of Article 65 or with the requirements of Article 66.[2] The amount of the periodical payment may vary in the course of the contingency, subject to the average rate thereof complying with these requirements.

Article 51

The benefit specified in Articles 49 and 50 shall, in a contingency covered, be secured at least to a woman in the classes protected who has completed such qualifying period as may be considered necessary to preclude abuse, and the benefit specified in Article 49 shall also be secured to the wife of a man in the classes protected where the latter has completed such qualifying period.

Article 52

The benefit specified in Articles 49 and 50 shall be granted throughout the contingency, except that the periodical payment may be limited to 12 weeks, unless a longer period of abstention from work is required or authorised by national laws or regulations, in which event it may not be limited to a period less than such longer period.

. . . .

(1 and 2)   Maternity Protection Convention (Revised), 1952 (No. 103)

. . . .

Article 1

1. This Convention applies to women employed in industrial undertakings and in non-industrial and agricultural occupations, including women wage earners working at home.

Standards and policy statements of special interest to women workers

2. For the purpose of this Convention, the term "industrial undertaking" comprises public and private undertakings and any branch thereof and includes particularly–

(a) mines, quarries, and other works for the extraction of minerals from the earth;
(b) undertakings in which articles are manufactured, altered, cleaned, repaired, ornamented, finished, adapted for sale, broken up or demolished, or in which materials are transformed, including undertakings engaged in shipbuilding, or in the generation, transformation or transmission of electricity or motive power of any kind;
(c) undertakings engaged in building and civil engineering work, including constructional, repair, maintenance, alteration and demolition work;
(d) undertakings engaged in the transport of passengers or goods by road, rail, sea, inland waterway or air, including the handling of goods at docks, quays, wharves, warehouses or airports.

3. For the purpose of this Convention, the term "non-industrial occupations" includes all occupations which are carried on in or in connection with the following undertakings or services, whether public or private:

(a) commercial establishments;
(b) postal and telecommunication services;
(c) establishments and administrative services in which the persons employed are mainly engaged in clerical work;
(d) newspaper undertakings;
(e) hotels, boarding houses, restaurants, clubs, cafés and other refreshment houses;
(f) establishments for the treatment and care of the sick, infirm or destitute and of orphans;
(g) theatres and places of public entertainment;
(h) domestic work for wages in private households;

and any other non-industrial occupations to which the competent authority may decide to apply the provisions of the Convention.

4. For the purpose of this Convention, the term "agricultural occupations" includes all occupations carried on in agricultural undertakings, including plantations and large-scale industrialised agricultural undertakings.

5. In any case in which it is doubtful whether this Convention applies to an undertaking, branch of an undertaking or occupation, the question shall be determined by the competent authority after consultation with the representative organisations of employers and workers concerned where such exist.

6. National laws or regulations may exempt from the application of this Convention undertakings in which only members of the employer's family, as defined by national laws or regulations, are employed.

Article 2

For the purpose of this Convention, the term "woman" means any female person, irrespective of age, nationality, race or creed, whether married or unmarried, and the term "child" means any child whether born of marriage or not.

Article 3

1. A woman to whom this Convention applies shall, on the production of a medical certificate stating the presumed date of her confinement, be entitled to a period of maternity leave.

2. The period of maternity leave shall be at least twelve weeks, and shall include a period of compulsory leave after confinement.

3. The period of compulsory leave after confinement shall be prescribed by national laws or regulations, but shall in no case be less than six weeks; the remainder of the total period of maternity leave may be provided before the presumed date of confinement or following expiration of the compulsory leave period or partly before the presumed date of confinement and partly following the expiration of the compulsory leave period as may be prescribed by national laws or regulations.

4. The leave before the presumed date of confinement shall be extended by any period elapsing between the presumed date of confinement and the actual date of confinement and the period of compulsory leave to be taken after confinement shall not be reduced on that account.

5. In case of illness medically certified arising out of pregnancy, national laws or regulations shall provide for additional leave before confinement, the maximum duration of which may be fixed by the competent authority.

6. In case of illness medically certified arising out of confinement, the woman shall be entitled to an extension of the leave after confinement, the maximum duration of which may be fixed by the competent authority.

Article 4

1. While absent from work on maternity leave in accordance with the provisions of Article 3, the woman shall be entitled to receive cash and medical benefits.

2. The rates of cash benefit shall be fixed by national laws or regulations so as to ensure benefits sufficient for the full and healthy maintenance of herself and her child in accordance with a suitable standard of living.

3. Medical benefits shall include prenatal, confinement and postnatal care by qualified midwives or medical practitioners as well as hospitalisation care where necessary; freedom of choice of doctor and freedom of choice between a public and private hospital shall be respected.

4. The cash and medical benefits shall be provided either by means of compulsory social insurance or by means of public funds; in either case they shall be provided as a matter of right to all women who comply with the prescribed conditions.

5. Women who fail to qualify for benefits provided as a matter of right shall be entitled, subject to the means test required for social assistance, to adequate benefits out of social assistance funds.

6. Where cash benefits provided under compulsory social insurance are based on previous earnings, they shall be at a rate of not less than two-thirds of the woman's previous earnings taken into account for the purpose of computing benefits.

7. Any contribution due under a compulsory social insurance scheme providing maternity benefits and any tax based upon payrolls which is raised for the purpose of providing such benefits shall, whether paid both by the employer and the employees or by the employer, be paid in respect of the total number of men and women employed by the undertakings concerned, without distinction of sex.

8. In no case shall the employer be individually liable for the cost of such benefits due to women employed by him.

Article 5

1. If a woman is nursing her child she shall be entitled to interrupt her work for this purpose at a time or times to be prescribed by national laws or regulations.

2. Interruptions of work for the purpose of nursing are to be counted as working hours and remunerated accordingly in cases in which the matter is governed by or in accordance with laws and regulations: in cases in which the matter is governed by collective agreement, the position shall be as determined by the relevant agreement.

Article 6

While a woman is absent from work on maternity leave in accordance with the provisions of Article 3 of this Convention, it shall not be lawful for her employer to give her notice of dismissal during such absence, or to give her notice of dismissal at such a time that the notice would expire during such absence.

Article 7

1. Any Member of the International Labour Organisation which ratifies this Convention may, by a declaration accompanying its ratification, provide for exceptions from the application of the Convention in respect of—

(a) certain categories of non-industrial occupations;
(b) occupations carried on in agricultural undertakings, other than plantations;
(c) domestic work for wages in private households;
(d) women wage earners working at home;
(e) undertakings engaged in the transport of passengers or goods by sea.

2. The categories of occupations or undertakings in respect of which the Member proposes to have recourse to the provisions of paragraph 1 of this Article shall be specified in the declaration accompanying its ratification.

3. Any Member which has made such a declaration may at any time cancel that declaration, in whole or in part, by a subsequent declaration.

4. Every Member for which a declaration made under paragraph 1 of this Article is in force shall indicate each year in its annual report upon the application of this Convention the position of its law and practice in respect of the occupations or undertakings to which paragraph 1 of this Article applies in virtue of the said declaration and the extent to which effect has been given or is proposed to be given to the Convention in respect of such occupations or undertakings.

. . . .

(1) Maternity Protection Recommendation, 1952 (No. 95)

. . . .

I. Maternity Leave

1. (1) Where necessary to the health of the woman and wherever practicable, the maternity leave provided for in Article 3, paragraph 2, of the Maternity Protection Convention (Revised), 1952, should be extended to a total period of 14 weeks.

(2) The supervisory bodies should have power to prescribe in individual cases, on the basis of a medical certificate, a further extension of the antenatal and postnatal leave provided for in paragraphs 4, 5 and 6 of Article 3 of the Maternity Protection Convention (Revised), 1952, if such an extension seems necessary for safeguarding the health of the mother and the child, and, in particular, in the event of actual or threatening abnormal conditions, such as miscarriage and other antenatal and postnatal complications.

Standards and policy statements of special interest to women workers

II. Maternity Benefits

2. (1) Wherever practicable the cash benefits to be granted in conformity with Article 4 of the Maternity Protection Convention (Revised), 1952, should be fixed at a higher rate than the minimum standard provided in the Convention, equalling, where practicable, 100 per cent of the woman's previous earnings taken into account for the purpose of computing benefits.

(2) Wherever practicable the medical benefits to be granted in conformity with article 4 of the said Convention should comprise general practitioner and specialist out-patient and in-patient care, including domiciliary visiting; dental care; the care given by qualified midwives and other maternity services at home or in hospital; nursing care at home or in hospital or other medical institutions; maintenance in hospitals or other medical institutions; pharmaceutical, dental or other medical or surgical supplies; and the care furnished under appropriate medical supervision by members of such other profession as may at any time be legally recognised as competent to furnish services associated with maternity care.

(3) The medical benefit should be afforded with a view to maintaining, restoring or improving the health of the woman protected and her ability to work and to attend to her personal needs.

(4) The institutions or government departments administering the medical benefit should encourage the women protected, by such means as may be deemed appropriate, to avail themselves of the general health services placed at their disposal by the public authorities or by other bodies recognised by the public authorities.

(5) In addition, national laws or regulations may authorise such institutions or government departments to make provision for the promotion of the health of the women protected and their infants.

(6) Other benefits in kind or in cash, such as layettes or payment for the purchase of layettes, the supply of milk or of nursing allowance for nursing mothers, etc., might be usefully added to the benefits mentioned in subparagraphs (1) and (2) of this paragraph.

III. Facilities for Nursing Mothers and Infants

3. (1) Wherever practicable nursing breaks should be extended to a total period of at least one-and-a-half hours during the working day and adjustments in the frequency and length of the nursing periods should be permitted on production of a medical certificate.

(2) Provision should be made for the establishment of facilities for nursing or day care, preferably outside the undertakings where the women are working; wherever possible provision should be made for the financing or at

least subsidising of such facilities at the expense of the community or by compulsory social insurance.

(3) The equipment and hygienic requirements of the facilities for nursing and day care and the number and qualifications of the staff of the latter should comply with adequate standards laid down by appropriate regulations, and they should be approved and supervised by the competent authority.

IV. Protection of Employment

4. (1) Wherever possible the period before and after confinement during which the woman is protected from dismissal by the employer in accordance with Article 6 of the Maternity Protection Convention (Revised), 1952, should be extended to begin as from the date when the employer of the woman has been notified by medical certificate of her pregnancy and to continue until one month at least after the end of the period of maternity leave provided for in Article 3 of the Convention.

(2) Among the legitimate reasons for dismissal during the protected period to be defined by law should be included cases of serious fault on the part of the employed woman, shutting down of the undertaking or expiry of the contract of employment. Where works councils exist it would be desirable that they should be consulted regarding such dismissals.

(3) During her legal absence from work before and after confinement, the seniority rights of the woman should be preserved as well as her right to reinstatement in her former work or in equivalent work paid at the same rate.

V. Protection of the Health of Employed Women during the Maternity Period

5. (1) Night work and overtime work should be prohibited for pregnant and nursing women and their working hours should be planned so as to ensure adequate rest periods.

(2) Employment of a woman on work prejudicial to her health or that of her child, as defined by the competent authority, should be prohibited during pregnancy and up to at least three months after confinement and longer if the woman is nursing her child.

(3) Work falling under the provisions of subparagraph (2) should include, in particular–

(a) any hard labour involving–
  (i) heavy weight-lifting, pulling or pushing; or
  (ii) undue and unaccustomed physical strain, including prolonged standing;

(b) work requiring special equilibrium; and

(c) work with vibrating machines.

(4) A woman ordinarily employed at work defined as prejudicial to health by the competent authority should be entitled without loss of wages to a transfer to another kind of work not harmful to her health.

(5) Such a right of transfer should also be given for reasons of maternity in individual cases to any woman who presents a medical certificate stating that a change in the nature of her work is necessary in the interest of her health and that of her child.

Resolution concerning Maternity Protection, adopted by the International Labour Conference at its 48th Session (Geneva, 1964)

The General Conference of the International Labour Organisation,

Considering that maternity protection is an obligation of society and cannot be a ground of discrimination in other fields relating to the employment of women,

Noting that few countries have ratified the Maternity Protection Convention, 1919, and that only eight have ratified the Maternity Protection Convention (Revised), 1952,

Noting in addition the studies and research undertaken by the International Labour Office both in countries which have ratified the Conventions and on those which have not ratified them;

1. Appeals to member States to take all possible measures to guarantee the application of these provisions to all women workers;

. . . .

Texts adopted by ILO Regional Conferences

Resolution concerning the Employment of Women and the Protection of Maternity, adopted by the Preparatory Asian Regional Conference (New Delhi, 1947)

. . . .

1. The protection of maternity and promotion of the welfare of women workers is a matter of vital and special importance to all the peoples of Asia because of the low standards of life, lack of education and widespread employment of women on heavy labour which characterise many of these countries and peoples.

. . . .

3. The Conference therefore requests the Governing Body to call the attention of the Governments of the Asian countries to the following measures for improving the position of the women workers in the countries

A. Maternity Protection

4. The protection of maternity in accordance with the principles adopted by the Committee on Social Security should cover as many categories of women workers as is administratively feasible, including women in all forms of heavy labour not excepting those employed in large-scale agriculture, such as plantations.

5. Pregnant women and nursing mothers should not be dismissed for that reason; and if the work performed by a pregnant woman or a nursing mother is prejudicial to her health, she should be allowed every facility for a change of work.

6. Children's crèches and day nurseries should be established in expanding numbers, so that the infants and children under school age of working women may be looked after in healthy and safe conditions. The crèches or day nurseries should be located with due regard to the convenience of mother and child, and should be under the direction and supervision of the competent public authority, which should wherever possible utilise the experience and facilities of existing institutions providing such services. Such services should be staffed by trained and qualified persons whose remuneration and conditions of employment should be such as to secure adequate and suitable personnel.

7. Additional social services such as canteens, and provision of milk, essential clothing and layettes should be made available for mother and child as far as practicable from public funds or at low cost.

. . . .

Resolution on Labour Policy, adopted by the Regional Meeting for the Near and Middle East (Istanbul, 1947)

. . . .

V. The Employment of Women and the Protection of Maternity

35. The promotion of the welfare of women workers and the protection of maternity is an especially important problem in the countries of the Near and Middle East because of the lack of education among women, and the low standard of women's wages which characterises many of these peoples.

. . . .

37. The following means of improving the position of women workers merit consideration by the governments of the Near and Middle Eastern countries with a view to their progressive adoption in these countries.

A. Maternity Protection

38. The protection of maternity should cover as many categories of women workers as is administratively practicable.

39. Free medical care should be provided before and after childbirth and during confinement.

40. (1) Maternity leave should be granted for an appropriate period before and after childbirth to be prescribed by national laws and regulations.

(2) Maternity benefits should be given for a period to coincide with maternity leave and should be sufficient for the healthy maintenance of mother and child.

(3) Such benefits should be provided as soon as practicable from social insurance or public funds.

41. Pregnant women and nursing mothers should not be dismissed for that reason; and if the work performed by a pregnant woman or nursing mother is prejudicial to her health she should be allowed every facility for a change of work.

42 (1) Children's crèches and day nurseries and social services such as canteens, provision of milk and essential clothing should be made available to mother and child as far as practicable.

(2) A woman who is nursing her child should be allowed half an hour twice a day during her working hours for this purpose.

B. Other Measures of Protection for Women Workers

43. In view of the special need to protect the health of women in order to ensure proper maternity protection the following measures should be adopted:

(a) the employment of women in dangerous or harmful occupations should be prohibited or regulated in accordance with national laws and regulations;

(b) weights to be lifted, carried, loaded or unloaded should be regulated by national laws or regulations with due regard to the physique of the worker, the method employed in lifting and carrying and the conditions of work;

(c) adequate and suitable accommodation in workplaces should be provided to serve as wash rooms, toilets, dressing rooms, etc.;

(d) adequate seating accommodation in workplaces should be provided for women for work or rest.

. . . .

SURVIVORS' BENEFIT

Texts adopted by the International Labour Conference

(1) Social Security (Minimum Standards) Convention, 1952 (No. 102)

. . . .

PART I. GENERAL PROVISIONS

Article 1

1. In this Convention—

(a) the term "prescribed" means determined by or in virtue of national laws or regulations;

(b) the term "residence" means ordinary residence in the territory of the Member and the term "resident" means a person ordinarily resident in the territory of the Member;

(c) the term "wife" means a wife who is maintained by her husband;

(d) the term "widow" means a woman who was maintained by her husband at the time of his death;

(e) the term "child" means a child under school-leaving age or under 15 years of age, as may be prescribed;

(f) the term "qualifying period" means a period of contribution, or a period of employment, or a period of residence, or any combination thereof, as may be prescribed.

. . . .

PART VI. EMPLOYMENT INJURY BENEFIT

Article 31

Each Member for which this Part of this Convention is in force shall secure to the persons protected the provision of employment injury benefit in accordance with the following Articles of this Part.

Article 32

The contingencies covered shall include the following where due to accident or a prescribed disease resulting from employment:

. . . .

(d) the loss of support suffered by the widow or child as the result of the death of the breadwinner; in the case of a widow, the right to benefit may be made conditional on her being presumed, in accordance with national laws or regulations, to be incapable of self-support.

Standards and policy statements of special interest to women workers

Article 33

The persons protected shall comprise–

(a) prescribed classes of employees, constituting not less than 50 per cent of all employees, and, for benefit in respect of death of the breadwinner, also their wives and children; or

(b) where a declaration made in virtue of Article 3³ is in force, prescribed classes of employees, constituting not less than 50 per cent of all employees in industrial workplaces employing 20 persons or more, and, for benefit in respect of death of the breadwinner, also their wives and children.

. . . .

PART X. SURVIVORS' BENEFIT

Article 59

Each Member for which this Part of this Convention is in force shall secure to the persons protected the provision of survivors' benefit in accordance with the following Articles of this Part.

Article 60

1. The contingency covered shall include the loss of support suffered by the widow or child as the result of the death of the breadwinner; in the case of a widow, the right to benefit may be made conditional on her being presumed, in accordance with national laws or regulations, to be incapable of self-support.

2. National laws or regulations may provide that the benefit of a person otherwise entitled to it may be suspended if such person is engaged in any prescribed gainful activity or that the benefit, if contributory, may be reduced where the earnings of the beneficiary exceed a prescribed amount, and, if non-contributory, may be reduced where the earnings of the beneficiary or his other means or the two taken together exceed a prescribed amount.

Article 61

The persons protected shall comprise–

(a) the wives and the children of breadwinners in prescribed classes of employees, which classes constitute not less than 50 per cent of all employees; or

(b) the wives and the children of breadwinners in prescribed classes of the economically active population, which classes constitute not less than 20 per cent of all residents; or

(c) all resident widows and resident children who have lost their breadwinner and whose means during the contingency do not exceed limits prescribed in such a manner as to comply with the requirements of Article 67;[4] or

(d) where a declaration made in virtue of Article 3 is in force, the wives and the children of breadwinners in prescribed classes of employees, which classes constitute not less than 50 per cent of all employees in industrial workplaces employing 20 persons or more.

Article 62

The benefit shall be a periodical payment calculated as follows:

(a) where classes of employees or classes of the economically active population are protected, in such a manner as to comply either with the requirements of Article 65 or with the requirements of Article 66;[4]

(b) where all residents whose means during the contingency do not exceed prescribed limits are protected, in such a manner as to comply with the requirements of Article 67.

Article 63

1. The benefit specified in Article 62 shall, in a contingency covered, be secured at least–

(a) to a person protected whose breadwinner has completed, in accordance with prescribed rules, a qualifying period which may be 15 years of contribution or employment, or 10 years of residence; or

(b) where, in principle, the wives and children of all economically active persons are protected, to a person protected whose breadwinner has completed a qualifying period of three years of contribution and in respect of whose breadwinner, while he was of working age, the prescribed yearly average number of contributions has been paid.

2. Where the benefit referred to in paragraph 1 is conditional upon a minimum period of contribution or employment, a reduced benefit shall be secured at least–

(a) to a person protected whose breadwinner has completed, in accordance with prescribed rules, a qualifying period of five years of contribution or employment; or

(b) where, in principle, the wives and children of all economically active persons are protected, to a person protected whose breadwinner has completed a qualifying period of three years of contribution and in respect of whose breadwinner, while he was of working age, half the yearly average number of contributions prescribed in accordance with subparagraph (b) of paragraph 1 of this Article has been paid.

3. The requirements of paragraph 1 of this Article shall be deemed to be satisfied where a benefit calculated in conformity with the requirements

of Part XI but a percentage of ten points lower than shown in the Schedule appended to that Part for the standard beneficiary concerned is secured at least to a person protected whose breadwinner has completed, in accordance with prescribed rules, five years of contribution, employment or residence.

4. A proportional reduction of the percentage indicated in the Schedule appended to Part XI may be effected where the qualifying period for the benefit corresponding to the reduced percentage exceeds five years of contribution or employment but is less than 15 years of contribution or employment; a reduced benefit shall be payable in conformity with paragraph 2 of this Article.

5. In order that a childless widow presumed to be incapable of self-support may be entitled to a survivor's benefit, a minimum duration of the marriage may be required.

Article 64

The benefit specified in Articles 62 and 63 shall be granted throughout the contingency.

. . . .

Invalidity, Old-Age and Survivors' Benefits Convention, 1967 (No. 128)

. . . .

PART I. GENERAL PROVISIONS

Article 1[5]

In this Convention—

(a) the term "legislation" includes any social security rules as well as laws and regulations;

(b) the term "prescribed" means determined by or in virtue of national legislation;

(c) the term "industrial undertaking" includes all undertakings in the following branches of economic activity: mining and quarrying; manufacturing; construction; electricity, gas, water and sanitary services; and transport, storage and communication;

(d) the term "residence" means ordinary residence in the territory of the Member, and the term "resident" means a person ordinarily resident in the territory of the Member;

(e) the term "dependent" refers to a state of dependency which is presumed to exist in prescribed cases;

(f) the term "wife" means a wife who is dependent on her husband;

Social security

(g) the term "widow" means a woman who was dependent on her husband at the time of his death;

(h) the term "child" covers–

   (i) a child under school-leaving age or under 15 years of age, whichever is the higher; and

   (ii) a child under a prescribed age higher than that specified in clause (i) of this subparagraph and who is an apprentice or student or has a chronic illness or infirmity disabling him for any gainful activity, under prescribed conditions: Provided that this requirement shall be deemed to be met where national legislation defines the term so as to cover any child under an age appreciably higher than that specified in clause (i) of this subparagraph;

(i) the term "qualifying period" means a period of contribution, or a period of employment, or a period of residence, or any combination thereof, as may be prescribed;

(j) the terms "contributory benefits" and "non-contributory benefits" mean respectively benefits the grant of which depends or does not depend on direct financial participation by the persons protected or their employer or on a qualifying period of occupational activity.

. . . .

PART IV. SURVIVORS' BENEFIT

Article 20

Each Member for which this Part of this Convention is in force shall secure to the persons protected the provision of survivors' benefit in accordance with the following Articles of this Part.

Article 21

1. The contingency covered shall include the loss of support suffered by the widow or child as the result of the death of the breadwinner.

2. In the case of a widow the right to a survivors' benefit may be made conditional on the attainment of a prescribed age. Such age shall not be higher than the age prescribed for old-age benefit.

3. No requirement as to age may be made if the widow–

(a) is invalid, as may be prescribed; or

(b) is caring for a dependent child of the deceased.

4. In order that a widow who is without a child may be entitled to a survivors' benefit, a minimum duration of marriage may be required.

Standards and policy statements of special interest to women workers

Article 22

1. The persons protected shall comprise–

(a) the wives, children and, as may be prescribed, other dependants of all breadwinners who were employees or apprentices; or
(b) the wives, children and, as may be prescribed, other dependants of breadwinners in prescribed classes of the economically active population, which classes constitute not less than 75 per cent of the whole economically active population; or
(c) all widows, all children and all other prescribed dependants who have lost their breadwinner, who are residents and, as appropriate, whose means during the contingency do not exceed limits prescribed in such a manner as to comply with the provisions of Article 28.

2. Where a declaration made in virtue of Article 4[6] is in force, the persons protected shall comprise–

(a) the wives, children and, as may be prescribed, other dependants of breadwinners in prescribed classes of employees, which classes constitute not less than 25 per cent of all employees; or
(b) the wives, children and, as may be prescribed, other dependants of breadwinners in prescribed classes of employees in industrial undertakings, which classes constitute not less than 50 per cent of all employees in industrial undertakings.

Article 23

1. The survivors' benefit shall be a periodical payment calculated as follows:

(a) where employees or classes of the economically active population are protected, in such a manner as to comply either with the requirements of Article 26 or with the requirements of Article 27;
(b) where all residents or all residents whose means during the contingency do not exceed prescribed limits are protected, in such a manner as to comply with the requirements of Article 28.

2. Acceptance of the obligations of this Convention shall, on condition that no declaration under Article 38 is in force, be deemed to constitute acceptance of the obligations of the following parts of the Social Security (Minimum Standards) Convention, 1952, and the relevant provisions of other Parts thereof, for the purpose of Article 2 of the said Convention:

. . . .

(c) Part X where the Member has accepted the obligations of this Convention in respect of Part IV.

Article 24

1. The benefit specified in Article 23 shall, in a contingency covered, be secured at least–

(a) to a person protected whose breadwinner has completed, in accordance with prescribed rules, a qualifying period which may be 15 years of contribution or employment, or ten years of residence: Provided that, for a benefit payable to a widow, the completion of a prescribed qualifying period of residence by such widow may be required instead; or

(b) where, in principle, the wives and children of all economically active persons are protected, to a person protected whose breadwinner has completed, in accordance with prescribed rules, a qualifying period of three years of contribution and in respect of whose breadwinner while he was of working age, the prescribed yearly average number or the yearly number of contributions has been paid.

2. Where the survivors' benefit is conditional upon a minimum period of contribution or employment, a reduced benefit shall be secured at least—

(a) to a person protected whose breadwinner has completed, in accordance with prescribed rules, a qualifying period of five years of contribution or employment; or

(b) where, in principle, the wives and children of all economically active persons are protected, to a person protected whose breadwinner has completed, in accordance with prescribed rules, a qualifying period of three years of contribution and in respect of whose breadwinner, while he was of working age, half of the yearly average number or of the yearly number of contributions prescribed in accordance with subparagraph *(b)* of paragraph 1 of this Article has been paid.

3. The requirements of paragraph 1 of this Article shall be deemed to be satisfied where a benefit calculated in conformity with the requirements of Part V but at a percentage of ten points lower than shown in the Schedule appended to that Part for the standard beneficiary concerned is secured at least to a person protected whose breadwinner has completed, in accordance with prescribed rules, five years of contribution, employment or residence.

4. A proportional reduction of the percentage indicated in the Schedule appended to Part V may be effected where the qualifying period for the benefit corresponding to the reduced percentage exceeds five years of contribution, employment or residence but is less than 15 years of contribution or employment or ten years of residence; if such qualifying period is one of contribution or employment, a reduced benefit shall be payable in conformity with paragraph 2 of this Article.

5. The requirements of paragraphs 1 and 2 of this Article shall be deemed to be satisfied where a benefit calculated in conformity with the requirements of Part V is secured at least to a person protected whose breadwinner has completed, in accordance with prescribed rules, a qualifying period of contribution or employment which shall not be more than five years at a prescribed minimum age and may rise with advancing age to not more than a prescribed maximum number of years.

Article 25

The benefit specified in Articles 23 and 24 shall be granted throughout the contingency.

(1) Invalidity, Old-Age and Survivors' Benefits Recommendation, 1967 (No. 131)

. . . .

II. PERSONS PROTECTED

. . . .

3. Members should extend the application of their legislation providing for survivors' benefits, by stages if necessary, and under appropriate conditions, to the wives, children and, as may be prescribed, other dependants of—

(a) persons whose employment is of a casual nature;
(b) all economically active persons.

III. CONTINGENCIES COVERED

. . . .

9. Where the widow's right to a survivors' benefit is conditional on the attainment of a prescribed age, a widow below that age should be given every assistance and all facilities, including training and placement facilities and the provision of benefit where appropriate, to enable her to obtain suitable employment.

10. A widow whose husband had fulfilled the prescribed qualifying conditions, but who does not herself fulfil the conditions for a survivors' benefit, should be entitled to an allowance for a specified period, or a lump-sum death benefit.

11. A contributory old-age benefit, or a contributory survivors' benefit payable to a widow, should not be suspended after a prescribed age solely because the person concerned is gainfully occupied.

12. An invalid and dependent widower should, under prescribed conditions, enjoy the same entitlements to survivors' benefit as a widow.

. . . .

19. A survivors' benefit should be secured at least on the qualifying conditions provided for in Paragraph 13[7] of this Recommendation for an invalidity benefit.

20. Where the grant of invalidity, old-age and survivors' benefits depends on a period of contribution or employment, at least periods of incapacity due to sickness, accident or maternity and periods of involuntary

unemployment, in respect of which benefit was paid, should be assimilated, under prescribed conditions, to periods of contribution or employment in calculating the qualifying period that has been fulfilled by the person concerned.

. . . .

Notes

[1] Under Article 3 a Member whose economy and medical facilities are insufficiently developed may, if and for so long as the competent authority considers necessary, avail itself, by a declaration appended to its ratification, of the temporary exception provided for in Article 48 *(c)*.

[2] Articles 65 and 66 concern standards to be complied with by periodical payments.

[3] Under Article 3.1. *(a)* a Member whose economy and medical facilities are insufficiently developed may, if and for so long as the competent authority considers necessary, avail itself, by a declaration appended to its ratification, of the temporary exceptions provided for in Article 33 *(b)*.

Each Member which has made a declaration under paragraph 1 of this Article shall include in the annual report upon the application of this Convention submitted under article 22 of the Constitution of the International Labour Organisation a statement, in respect of each exception of which it avails itself–

(a) that its reason for doing so subsists; or

(b) that it renounces its right to avail itself of the exception in question as from a stated date.

[4] Articles 65, 66 and 67 concern standards to be complied with by periodical payments.

[5] Similar provisions are contained in paragraph 1 of the Invalidity, Old-Age and Survivors' Benefits Recommendation, 1967 (No. 131), on page 104.

[6] In conformity with the provisions of Article 75 of the Social Security (Minimum Standards) Convention, 1952, the following Parts of that Convention and the relevant provisions of other Parts thereof shall cease to apply to any Member having ratified this Convention as from the date at which this Convention is binding on that Member and no declaration under Article 38 is in force:

. . . .

(c) Part X where the Member has accepted the obligations of this Convention in respect of Part IV.

[7] 13. An invalidity benefit should be secured at least to a person protected who has completed, prior to the contingency, in accordance with prescribed rules, a qualifying period which may be five years of contribution, employment or residence.

INDUSTRIAL RELATIONS 5

Texts adopted by the International Labour Conference

(1) Freedom of Association and Protection of the Right to Organise Convention, 1948 (No. 87)

. . . .

PART I. FREEDOM OF ASSOCIATION

. . . .

Article 2

Workers and employers, without distinction whatsoever, shall have the right to establish and, subject only to the rules of the organisation concerned, to join organisations of their own choosing without previous authorisation.

. . . .

(1) Rural Workers' Organisations Convention, 1975 (No. 141)

. . . .

Article 4[1]

It shall be an objective of national policy concerning rural development to facilitate the establishment and growth, on a voluntary basis, of strong and independent organisations of rural workers as an effective means of ensuring the participation of rural workers, without discrimination as defined in the Discrimination (Employment and Occupation) Convention, 1958, in economic and social development in the benefits resulting therefrom.

. . . .

(1) Rural Workers' Organisations Recommendation, 1975 (No. 149)

. . . .

C. Education and Training

16. In order to ensure a sound growth of rural workers' organisations and the rapid assumption of their full role in economic and social development, steps should be taken, by the competent authority among others, to—

. . . .

(c) promote programmes directed to the role which women can and should play in the rural community, integrated in general programmes of education and training to which women and men should have equal opportunities of access;

. . . .

17. (1) As an effective means of providing the training and education referred to in Paragraph 16, programmes of workers' education or adult education, specially adapted to national and local conditions and to the social, economic and cultural needs of the various categories of rural workers, including the special needs of women and young persons, should be formulated and applied.

. . . .

(1) Consultation (Industrial and National Levels) Recommendation, 1960 (No. 113)

. . . .

1. (1) Measures appropriate to national conditions should be taken to promote effective consultation and co-operation at the industrial and national levels between public authorities and employers' and workers' organisations, as well as between these organisations, for the purposes indicated in Paragraphs 4 and 5 below, and on such other matters of mutual concern as the parties may determine.

(2) Such measures should be applied without discrimination of any kind against these organisations or amongst them on grounds such as the race, sex, religion, political opinion or national extraction of their members.

. . . .

4. Such consultation and co-operation should have the general objective of promoting mutual understanding and good relations between public authorities and employers' and workers' organisations, as well as between these organisations, with a view to developing the economy as a whole or individual branches thereof, improving conditions of work and raising standards of living.

5. Such consultation and co-operation should aim, in particular—

(a) at joint consideration by employers' and workers' organisations of matters of mutual concern with a view to arriving, to the fullest possible extent, at agreed solutions; and

(b) at ensuring that the competent public authorities seek the views, advice

and assistance of employers' and workers' organisations in an appropriate manner, in respect of such matters as—
  (i) the preparation and implementation of laws and regulations affecting their interests;
  (ii) the establishment and functioning of national bodies, such as those responsible for organisation of employment, vocational training and retraining, labour protection, industrial health and safety, productivity, social security and welfare; and
  (iii) the elaboration and implementation of plans of economic and social development.

Text adopted by an ILO Regional Conference

Resolution concerning the Employment and Conditions of Work of Women in African Countries, adopted by the Second African Regional Conference of the ILO (Addis Ababa, 1964)

. . . .

14. Women should be entitled to join trade unions of their choice freely and should have the possibility of occupying responsible posts in the unions and of obtaining adequate training for this purpose.

. . . .

19. In the consideration and formulation of policy regarding the employment of women there should be consultation and co-operation between public authorities and employers' and workers' organisations at all appropriate levels. Women representatives should take part in consultations to the maximum extent possible.

. . . .

Texts adopted by ILO Industrial Meetings, etc.

Resolution on Industrial Relations in Inland Transport, adopted by the Inland Transport Committee at its 2nd Session (Geneva, 1947)

. . . .

1. FREEDOM OF ASSOCIATION

1. Employers and workers, whether in public or private inland transport undertakings, should be entitled to form, without previous authorisation and without restriction of occupation, sex, colour, race, creed or nationality, organisations of their own choosing.

. . . .

Standards and policy statements of special interest to women workers

Resolution concerning Industrial Relations in the Metal Trades, adopted by the Metal Trades Committee at its 1st Session (Toledo, Ohio, 1946)

. . . .

The Metal Trades Committee of the International Labour Organisation,

. . . .

Considers that at the present time it is opportune to recall one of the fundamental principles of the Declaration of Philadephia, the Charter of the International Labour Organisation, which proclaims freedom of expression and the right of association.

This principle implies for the employers and workers of the metal trades the absolute right to form themselves freely into organisations, whether federations or confederations, without previous authorisation, or to join the organisation which they prefer. This absolute right should extend to all, without distinction of sex, race or religious belief, and its exercise should not involve victimisation.

. . . .

Note

[1] A similar provision is contained in Paragraph 4 of the Rural Workers' Organisations Recommendation, 1975 (No. 149), below.

SELECTED CATEGORIES OF WORKERS

6

DOMESTIC WORKERS

Texts adopted by the International Labour Conference

Resolution concerning the Conditions of Employment of Domestic Workers, adopted by the International Labour Conference at its 49th Session (Geneva, 1965)

The General Conference of the International Labour Organisation,

Considering that in a number of member countries, both developed and developing, domestic workers in many cases are either not protected at all or only insufficiently by legislation or other provisions concerning their working and living conditions,

Considering the urgent need to provide for domestic workers in all member countries the basic elements of protection which would assure to them a minimum standard of living, compatible with the self-respect and human dignity which are essential to social justice,

Considering that in many member countries a considerable lack of experience exists in establishing minimum standards of working conditions in domestic employment,

. . . .

1. Urges member States to make all practicable efforts to promote the introduction of protective measures for domestic workers, such as hours of work and other conditions of employment, as well as the training of such workers in accordance with International Labour Organisation standards.

. . . .

Standards and policy statements of special interest to women workers

HOME WORKERS

Text adopted by an ILO Regional Conference

Resolution concerning Home Work, adopted by the Second Conference of American States Members (Havana, 1939)

The Committee on the Work of Women and Juveniles, having approved a number of principles concerning the protection of the wages of women employed in home work, and wishing at the same time to indicate what are, in its opinion, the general lines for a social policy with regard to home work with the object of improving the position of the workers employed in it, most of whom are women;

Decides to formulate its opinion in the following terms:

1. Industrial home work on behalf of an outside employer should be abolished in the American countries as a form of production as being against the interests of the workers and of the national economic system.

2. So long as industrial home work continues to exist, the necessary legal measures should be adopted to prevent it from being a means of defrauding the interests of the State or of slowing down the development of technical progress in industry, and also to ensure to home workers effective protection, extending to them social legislation and the benefit of social insurance schemes. Investigations should be carried out to determine a policy for the regulation of home work, and a sufficiently energetic system of supervision should be established to prevent breaches of the law.

Texts adopted by ILO Industrial Meetings, etc.

Resolution (No. 2) concerning Industrial Home Work in the Clothing Industry, adopted by the Tripartite Technical Meeting for the Clothing Industry (Geneva, 1964)

. . . .

Considering that low wages, long hours, unhealthy sanitary conditions and inadequate safety standards for industrial homeworkers can threaten the labour and employment conditions of clothing workers generally,

Considering that industrial home work is in such cases a source of unfair competition on the part of employers who evade decent labour standards and who shift to the homeworker such costs as those of rent, light, heat and of the machine,

Considering that, although these undesirable practices may gradually vanish as the manufacture of ready-made clothing becomes more industrialised, such home work is damaging to the workers concerned and to the image of the bona fide clothing industry, and

Selected categories of workers

Considering that there are inherent difficulties in effectively controlling industrial home work;

. . . .

1. Industrial home work in the clothing industry should, as a matter of principle, ultimately be abolished, except as to certain individuals–for example physically handicapped persons–who cannot adapt themselves to factory work.

2. Where it is not yet practicable to eliminate home work from the clothing industry, governmental regulations–including registration of homeworkers, agents and employers–should be strictly applied in an attempt to ensure that labour conditions and social security standards of industrial homeworkers are to the maximum possible extent identical with those of factory workers.

Conclusions (No. 1) concerning the Effects of Technological Developments on the Occupational Structure and Level of Employment in the Leather and Footwear Industry, adopted by the Tripartite Technical Meeting for the Leather and Footwear Industry (Geneva, 1969)

. . . .

15. In countries or sectors where home working by women is on a considerable scale, its reduction would be facilitated by a reorganisation of factory arrangements such as recourse to special working periods and the introduction of appropriate social benefits, actions designed to enable them to fulfil their responsibilities at home and at work.

. . . .

Conclusions concerning the Effects of Technological Progress on Working Conditions and Working Environment in the Leather and Footwear Industry, adopted by the Second Tripartite Technical Meeting for the Leather and Footwear Industry (Geneva, December 1979)

. . . .

HOME WORK

8. The need to improve the conditions of homeworkers implies concerted action by governments, employers and workers and their organisations. Such action should lead to an improvement in their situation and to better application of relevant legislation on such matters as contracts of employment, remuneration, safety and health, termination and social security. Homeworkers should receive wages and benefits equivalent to those paid to workers in industrial enterprises, who are engaged in similar work.

. . . .

Small-scale Industries and Home Work

23. In small-scale and cottage-level industries, whether manual or mechanised, strain and injury result from work posture (e.g. funnel chest) and monotony. Ergonomic improvements in the working environment are necessary to minimise the risks.

24. In situations where certain operations of tanning or footwear manufacture are undertaken as home work, all the members of the family are exposed to occupational hazards. Furthermore, exposure is not limited to working hours. Selection, by appropriate means, of particular operations for home work would minimise the risk. It is necessary to prohibit highly hazardous types of home work, or such work by self-employed persons through national legislation.

. . . .

Resolution concerning Industrial Home Work, adopted by the Second Tripartite Technical Meeting for the Leather and Footwear Industry (Geneva, December 1979)

. . . .

Considering the importance of industrial home work in some ILO member States, particularly as regards shoe, glove and fancy-leather goods manufacturing,

Noting that this type of work raises complex social problems, the most evident of which are frequent infringements of the standards laid down by legislation or by agreements on the protection of workers;

. . . .

The Second Tripartite Technical Meeting for the Leather and Footwear Industry:

(1) invites the Governing Body of the International Labour Office to request member States to take the following measures:

   (a) to regulate the conditions of industrial home work;

   (b) to establish the necessary controls over all forms of industrial home work;

. . . .

MIGRANT WORKERS

Texts adopted by the International Labour Conference

(1) Migration for Employment Convention (Revised), 1949 (No. 97)

. . . .

Article 6

1. Each Member for which this Convention is in force undertakes to apply, without discrimination in respect of nationality, race, religion or sex, to immigrants lawfully within its territory, treatment no less favourable than that which it applies to its own nationals in respect of the following matters:

(a) in so far as such matters are regulated by law or regulations, or are subject to the control of administrative authorities–
   (i) remuneration, including family allowances where these form part of remuneration, hours of work, overtime arrangements, holidays with pay, restrictions on home work, minimum age for employment, apprenticeship and training, women's work and the work of young persons;
   (ii) membership of trade unions and enjoyment of the benefits of collective bargaining;
   (iii) accommodation;

(b) social security (that is to say, legal provision in respect of employment injury, maternity, sickness, invalidity, old age, death, unemployment and family responsibilities, and any other contingency which, according to national laws or regulations, is covered by a social security scheme), subject to the following limitations:
   (i) there may be appropriate arrangements for the maintenance of acquired rights and rights in course of acquisition;
   (ii) national laws or regulations of immigration countries may prescribe special arrangements concerning benefits or portions of benefits which are payable wholly out of public funds, and concerning allowances paid to persons who do not fulfil the contribution conditions prescribed for the award of a normal pension;

. . . .

(1) Migration for Employment Recommendation (Revised), 1949 (No. 86)

. . . .

ANNEX

Model Agreement on Temporary and Permanent Migration for Employment, including Migration of Refugees and Displaced Persons

. . . .

ARTICLE 17. EQUALITY OF TREATMENT

1. The competent authority of the territory of immigration shall grant to migrants *and to members of their families* with respect to employment in which they are eligible to engage treatment no less favourable than that

applicable to its own nationals in virtue of legal or administrative provisions or collective labour agreements.

2. Such equality of treatment shall apply, without discrimination in respect of nationality, race, religion or sex, to immigrants lawfully within the territory of immigration in respect of the following matters:

(a) in so far as such matters are regulated by laws or regulations or are subject to the control of administrative authorities,
- (i) remuneration, including family allowances where these form part of remuneration, hours of work, weekly rest days, overtime arrangements, holidays with pay and other regulations concerning employment, including limitations on home work, minimum age provisions, women's work, and the work of young persons;
- (ii) membership of trade unions and enjoyment of the benefits of collective bargaining;
- (iii) admission to schools, to apprenticeship and to courses or schools for vocational or technical training, provided that this does not prejudice nationals of the country of immigration;
- (iv) recreation and welfare measures;

(b) employment taxes, dues or contributions payable in respect of the persons employed;

(c) hygiene, safety and medical assistance;

(d) legal proceedings relating to the matters referred to in this Agreement.

(1) Migrant Workers (Supplementary Provisions) Convention, 1975 (No. 143)

. . . .

PART II. EQUALITY OF OPPORTUNITY AND TREATMENT

Article 10

Each Member for which the Convention is in force undertakes to declare and pursue a national policy designed to promote and to guarantee, by methods appropriate to national conditions and practice, equality of opportunity and treatment in respect of employment and occupation, óf social security, of trade union and cultural rights and of individual and collective freedoms for persons who as migrant workers or as members of their families are lawfully within its territory.

. . . .

Article 12

Each Member shall, by methods appropriate to national conditions and practice–

. . . .

(e) in consultation with representative organisations of employers and workers, formulate and apply a social policy appropriate to national conditions and practice which enables migrant workers and their families to share in advantages enjoyed by its nationals while taking account, without adversely affecting the principle of equality of opportunity and treatment, of such special needs as they may have until they are adapted to the society of the country of employment;

. . . .

Article 13

1. A Member may take all necessary measures which fall within its competence and collaborate with other Members to facilitate the reunification of the families of all migrant workers legally residing in its territory.

2. The members of the family of the migrant worker to which this Article applies are the spouse and dependent children, father and mother.

. . . .

(1) Migrant Workers (Supplementary Provisions) Recommendation, 1975 (No. 151)

. . . .

I. EQUALITY OF OPPORTUNITY AND TREATMENT

2. Migrant workers and members of their families lawfully within the territory of a Member should enjoy effective equality of opportunity and treatment with nationals of the Member concerned in respect of–

(a) access to vocational guidance and placement services;

(b) access to vocational training and employment of their own choice on the basis of individual suitability for such training or employment, account being taken of qualifications acquired outside the territory of and in the country of employment;

(c) advancement in accordance with their individual character, experience, ability and diligence;

(d) security of employment, the provision of alternative employment, relief work and retraining;

(e) remuneration for work of equal value;

(f) conditions of work, including hours of work, rest periods, annual holidays with pay, occupational safety and occupational health measures, as well as social security measures and welfare facilities and benefits provided in connection with employment;

(g) membership of trade unions, exercise of trade union rights and eligibility for office in trade unions and in labour-management relations bodies, including bodies representing workers in undertakings;

Standards and policy statements of special interest to women workers

(h) rights of full membership in any form of co-operative;
(i) conditions of life, including housing and the benefits of social services and educational and health facilities.

. . . .

II. SOCIAL POLICY

9. Each Member should, in consultation with representative organisations of employers and workers, formulate and apply a social policy appropriate to national conditions and practice which enables migrant workers and their families to share in advantages enjoyed by its nationals while taking account, without adversely affecting the principle of equality of opportunity and treatment, of such special needs as they may have until they are adapted to the society of the country of employment.

. . . .

NURSING PERSONNEL

Texts adopted by the International Labour Conference

(1) Nursing Personnel Convention, 1977 (No. 149)

. . . .

Recognising the vital role played by nursing personnel, together with other workers in the field of health, in the protection and improvement of the health and welfare of the population, and

Recognising that the public sector as an employer of nursing personnel should play an active role in the improvement of conditions of employment and work of nursing personnel, and

Noting that the present situation of nursing personnel in many countries, in which there is a shortage of qualified persons and existing staff are not always utilised to best effect, is an obstacle to the development of effective health services, ... [1]

. . . .

Article 1

. . . .

2. This Convention applies to all nursing personnel, wherever they work.

. . . .

Article 6

Nursing personnel shall enjoy conditions at least equivalent to those of other workers in the country concerned in the following fields:

. . . .

(e) maternity leave;

. . . .

(1) Nursing Personnel Recommendation, 1977 (No. 157)

. . . .

VII. REMUNERATION

25. (1) The remuneration of nursing personnel should be fixed at levels which are commensurate with their socio-economic needs, qualifications, responsibilities, duties and experience, which take account of the constraints and hazards inherent in the profession, and which are likely to attract persons to the profession and retain them in it.

(2) Levels of remuneration should bear comparison with those of other professions requiring similar or equivalent qualifications and carrying similar or equivalent responsibilities.

(3) Levels of remuneration for nursing personnel having similar or equivalent duties and working in similar or equivalent conditions should be comparable, whatever the establishments, areas or sectors in which they work.

(4) Remuneration should be adjusted from time to time to take into account variations in the cost of living and rises in the national standard of living.

(5) The remuneration of nursing personnel should preferably be fixed by collective agreement.

26. Scales of remuneration should take account of the classification of functions and responsibilities recommended in Paragraphs 5 and 6 and of the principles of career policy set out in Paragraph 21 of this Recommendation.

27. Nursing personnel who work in particularly arduous or unpleasant conditions should receive financial compensation for this.

. . . .

VIII. WORKING TIME AND REST PERIODS

. . . .

40. Nursing personnel who work in particularly arduous or unpleasant

conditions should benefit from a reduction of working hours and/or an increase in rest periods, without any decrease in total remuneration.

. . . .

42. (1) Nursing personnel, without distinction between married and unmarried persons, should be assured the benefits and protection provided for in the Maternity Protection Convention (Revised), 1952, and the Maternity Protection Recommendation, 1952.

(2) Maternity leave should not be considered to be sick leave.

(3) The measures provided for in the Employment (Women with Family Responsibilities) Recommendation, 1965, should be applied in respect of nursing personnel.

43. In accordance with Paragraph 19 of this Recommendation, decisions concerning the organisation of work, working time and rest periods should be taken in agreement or in consultation with freely chosen representatives of the nursing personnel or with organisations representing them.

. . . .

IX. Occupational Health Protection

. . . .

50. Pregnant women and parents of young children whose normal assignment could be prejudicial to their health or that of their child should be transferred, without loss of entitlements, to work appropriate to their situation.

. . . .

ANNEX

Suggestions concerning Practical Application

. . . .

Remuneration

16. Pending the attainment of levels of remuneration comparable with those of other professions requiring similar or equivalent qualifications and carrying similar or equivalent responsibilities, measures should be taken, where necessary, to bring remuneration as rapidly as possible to a level which is likely to attract nursing personnel to the profession and retain them in it.

. . . .

Occupational Health Protection

. . . .

26. Work to which pregnant women or mothers of young children should not be assigned should include–

(a) as regards women covered by Paragraph 5 of the Maternity Protection Recommendation, 1952, the types of work enumerated therein;[2]
(b) generally, work involving exposure to ionising radiations or anaesthetic substances or involving contact with infectious diseases.

. . . .

Resolution concerning the Application of Certain International Labour Standards to Nursing Personnel, adopted by the International Labour Conference at its 63rd Session (Geneva, 1977)

The General Conference of the International Labour Organisation,

Recalling that nursing personnel are covered by many international labour Conventions and Recommendations laying down general standards concerning employment and conditions of work,

Noting, in particular, that–

. . . .

(b) the Discrimination (Employment and Occupation) Convention, 1958, is designed to promote equality of opportunity and treatment in every employment and occupation, and that the Equal Remuneration Convention, 1951, is designed to promote the application "to all workers" of the principle of equal remuneration;

. . . .

Appeals to all Members to ensure that the provisions of these and other relevant instruments are fully applied in practice to nursing personnel.

PLANTATIONS

Texts adopted by the International Labour Conference

(2) Plantations Convention, 1958 (No. 110)

. . . .

PART I. GENERAL PROVISIONS

. . . .

Article 2

Each Member which ratifies this Convention undertakes to apply its provisions equally to all plantation workers without distinction as to race, colour, sex, religion, political opinion, nationality, social origin, tribe or trade union membership.

. . . .

Standards and policy statements of special interest to women workers

PART II. ENGAGEMENT AND RECRUITMENT AND MIGRANT WORKERS

. . . .

Article 15

Where the families of recruited workers have been authorised to accompany the workers to the place of employment the competent authority shall take all necessary measures for safeguarding their health and welfare during the journey...

. . . .

Article 19

Each Member for which this Part of this Convention is in force undertakes to maintain, within its jurisdiction, appropriate medical services responsible for–

(a) ascertaining, where necessary, both at the time of departure and on arrival, that migrants for employment on a plantation and the members of their families authorised to accompany or join them are in reasonable health;
(b) ensuring that migrants for employment on a plantation and members of their families enjoy adequate medical attention and good hygienic conditions at the time of departure, during the journey and on arrival in the territory of destination.

. . . .

PART VII. MATERNITY PROTECTION

Article 46

For the purpose of this Part of this Convention, the term "woman" means any female person, irrespective of age, nationality, race or creed, whether married or unmarried, and the term "child" means any child whether born of marriage or not.

Article 47

1. A woman to whom this Part of this Convention applies shall, on the production of appropriate evidence of the presumed date of her confinement, be entitled to a period of maternity leave.

2. The competent authority may, after consultation with the most representative organisations of employers and workers, where such exist, prescribe a qualifying period for maternity leave which shall not exceed a total of 150 days of employment with the same employer during the 12 months preceding the confinement.

3. The period of maternity leave shall be at least 12 weeks, and shall include a period of compulsory leave after confinement.

4. The period of compulsory leave after confinement shall be prescribed by national laws or regulations, but shall in no case be less than six weeks; the remainder of the total period of maternity leave may be provided before the presumed date of confinement or following expiration of the compulsory leave period or partly before the presumed date of confinement and partly following the expiration of the compulsory leave period as may be prescribed by national laws or regulations.

5. The leave before the presumed date of confinement shall be extended by any period elapsing between the presumed date of confinement and the actual date of confinement, and the period of compulsory leave to be taken after confinement shall not be reduced on that account.

6. In case of illness suitably certified as arising out of pregnancy national laws or regulations shall provide for additional leave before confinement, the maximum duration of which may be fixed by the competent authority.

7. In case of illness suitably certified as arising out of confinement the woman shall be entitled to an extension of the leave after confinement, the maximum duration of which may be fixed by the competent authority.

8. No pregnant woman shall be required to undertake any type of work harmful to her in the period prior to her maternity leave.

Article 48

1. While absent from work on maternity leave in accordance with the provisions of Article 47, the woman shall be entitled to receive cash and medical benefits.

2. The rates of cash benefit shall be fixed by national laws or regulations so as to ensure benefits sufficient for the full and healthy maintenance of herself and her child in accordance with a suitable standard of living.

3. Medical benefits shall include prenatal, confinement and postnatal care by qualified midwives or medical practitioners as well as hospitalisation care where necessary; freedom of choice of doctor and freedom of choice between a public and private hospital shall be respected as far as practicable.

4. Any contribution due under a compulsory social insurance scheme providing maternity benefits and any tax based upon payrolls which is raised for the purpose of providing such benefits shall, whether paid both by the employer and the employees or by the employer, be paid in respect of the total number of men and women employed by the undertakings concerned, without distinction of sex.

Standards and policy statements of special interest to women workers

Article 49

1. If a woman is nursing her child she shall be entitled to interrupt her work for this purpose, under conditions to be prescribed by national laws or regulations.

2. Interruptions of work for the purpose of nursing are to be counted as working hours and remunerated accordingly in cases in which the matter is governed by or in accordance with laws and regulations; in cases in which the matter is governed by collective agreement, the position shall be as determined by the relevant agreement.

Article 50

1. While a woman is absent from work on maternity leave in accordance with the provisions of Article 47, it shall not be lawful for her employer to give her notice of dismissal during such absence, or to give her notice of dismissal at such a time that the notice would expire during such absence.

2. The dismissal of a woman solely because she is pregnant or a nursing mother shall be prohibited.

(2) Plantations Recommendation, 1958 (No. 110)

. . . .

IV. EQUAL REMUNERATION

27. (1) Each Member should, by means appropriate to the methods in operation for determining rates of remuneration, promote and, in so far as is consistent with such methods, ensure the application to all workers of the principle of equal remuneration for men and women workers for work of equal value.

(2) This principle may be applied by means of–

(a) national laws or regulations;
(b) legally established or recognised machinery for wage determination;
(c) collective agreements between employers and workers; or
(d) a combination of these various means.

. . . .

X. SOCIAL SECURITY

53. Each Member should extend its laws and regulations establishing systems of insurance or other appropriate systems providing security in case

Selected categories of workers

of sickness, maternity, invalidity, old age and similar social risks to plantation workers on conditions equivalent to those prevailing in the case of workers in industrial and commercial occupations.

. . . .

Texts adopted by ILO Industrial Meetings, etc.

Resolution (No. 40) concerning the Extension of Social Security to Plantation Workers and their Families, adopted by the Committee on Work on Plantations at its Fourth Session (Geneva, 1961)

. . . .

8. In view of the special nature of work on plantations, the workers should, in case of incapacity for work due to sickness or maternity, retain their right to the facilities normally provided. As regards housing, occupation should continue for a reasonable period of time in order to allow a satisfactory alternative dwelling to be provided.

. . . .

Conclusions (No. 51) concerning Practical Measures to Promote Good Labour-Management Relations on Plantations, adopted by the Committee on Work on Plantations at its 5th Session (Geneva, 1966)

. . . .

13. It is desirable for plantation managements to develop policies and procedures concerning recruitment and engagement aimed at the development of a stable labour force and of stable employment on plantations. Such policies should be based on the following principles:

. . . .

(b) there should be no discrimination on grounds of race, colour, sex, religion, political opinion, national extraction or social origin, in accordance with the Discrimination (Employment and Occupation) Convention, 1958;

(c) appropriate and equal opportunities should be given to women workers for appointment to posts for which they are qualified and for improving their qualifications and suitability for posts in all grades;

. . . .

Conclusions (No. 63) concerning Conditions of Work of Women and Young Workers on Plantations, adopted by the Committee on Work on Plantations at its 6th Session (Geneva, 1971)

I. EMPLOYMENT OPPORTUNITIES

. . . .

3. In some developing countries, owing to the fragmentation of holdings or the diversion of land to non-plantation purposes, the amount of land

available for plantation employment is decreasing while the number of persons dependent upon it is increasing.

4. These changes are adversely affecting the employment opportunities of all workers and, more particularly, those of women and young workers.

5. Measures to protect present employment and improve employment opportunities are therefore becoming more and more urgent.

6. Such measures must include, as a matter of high priority, the provision of adequate training facilities in places easily accessible to the plantation population. Care should be taken, however, to ensure that the training programmes established form an integral part of national development programmes and that the jobs for which training is offered actually do exist or will exist in the near future.

. . . .

10. To the maximum extent possible, employment should be offered to women, no less than to men, on a permanent basis. Non-permanent workers, on whatever basis they are recruited, having regard to the seasonal character of agricultural work, should be registered on an employment roll of the plantation and should have the same rights as other workers in respect of wages, hours of work and, to the extent that they qualify under the relevant legal or other provisions, holidays with pay, maternity leave and all other fringe benefits.

. . . .

12. Population pressures in some countries are intensifying employment difficulties and other social problems, such as housing, health and sanitation on plantations. They are also undermining the health of women and, by adding to the financial burden of wage earners, the well-being of families. Where appropriate to national conditions and consistent with national policies, family planning advice and assistance should be provided to plantation workers in a systematic and sustained manner. To ensure the effectiveness of their programmes, family planning agencies should enlist the co-operation of employers and trade unions. Trade unions should be helped in obtaining the material resources necessary to enable them to make the fullest possible contribution and more particularly, to reorient their educational programmes.

II. Wages and Working Conditions

13. All necessary measures should be taken to eliminate or prevent any discrimination against women in respect of wages, working conditions or employment. The provisions of the Discrimination (Employment and Occupation) Convention, 1958 (No. 111), and the Equal Remuneration Convention, 1951 (No. 100), should be fully implemented.

Selected categories of workers

14. Special attention should be paid, in the determination of incentive rates and tasks as well as time rates, to the effective application of the principle of equal pay for work of equal value. Differentials should be clearly based on an objective appreciation of considerations such as the difficulty of the job and the skills required rather than on sex or subjective distinctions.

15. In fixing wage rates, the employment of members of the family should not be taken into consideration. The wages should be fixed according to the work done.

. . . .

17. Hours of work of women should be fixed in conformity with laws or regulations and with due regard to their health and family responsibilities. Regardless of the method of remuneration, higher rates should be paid for overtime periods as defined in accordance with the national laws applicable in the plantations.

18. Efforts should be made to secure the application of national standards concerning wages, hours and other conditions of work especially to women and young workers employed in smallholdings.

19. Adequate and effective inspection is essential for the enforcement of laws and regulations concerning wages and conditions of work. In addition to verifying the observance of laws and regulations, inspectors should give valuable advice to employers and workers on their rights and responsibilities. To perform inspections with sufficient frequency and effectiveness, labour inspection services dealing with plantations must be strengthened and they should be staffed so as to be able to deal effectively with special problems of women, and young workers. Employers and trade unions should fully co-operate with labour inspectors to enable them to carry out their inquiries, and labour inspectors should actively seek such co-operation. Trade unions should offer their assistance to workers wishing to make representations for the protection of their rights.

III. LIVING CONDITIONS

. . . .

23. For workers employed at high altitudes or otherwise exposed to extremes of weather, adequate protective clothing should be provided. Workers exposed to other hazards, such as those arising from the use of chemicals or new types of machinery, should be protected by adequate safeguards. Special attention in this regard should be given to the particular vulnerability of women and young workers.

24. To minimise the risks connected with childbirth to the lives and health of women, as well as the risk of infant mortality, adequate prenatal, confinement and postnatal facilities, including the services of trained midwives, should be provided in plantations. Women workers and their hus-

bands should be educated in the importance of making full use of such facilities.

25. Adequate facilities should be provided for the care of children of working mothers. Such facilities should include suitable arrangements for supervision and nutrition. Working mothers should be given time off with pay to nurse their infants up to a specified age.

TEACHERS

Recommendation concerning the Status of Teachers, adopted by the Special Intergovernmental Conference on the Status of Teachers (Paris, 1966)

IV. GUIDING PRINCIPLES

7. All aspects of the preparation and employment of teachers should be free from any form of discrimination on grounds of race, colour, sex, religion, political opinion, national or social origin, or economic condition.

IV. Educational objectives and policies

10. Appropriate measures should be taken in each country to the extent necessary to formulate comprehensive educational policies consistent with the Guiding Principles, drawing on all available resources, human and otherwise. In so doing, the competent authorities should take account of the consequences for teachers of the following principles and objectives:

(b) all facilities should be made available equally to enable every person to enjoy his right to education without discrimination on grounds of sex, race, colour, religion, political opinion, national or social origin, or economic condition;

VII. EMPLOYMENT AND CAREER

Women Teachers with Family Responsibilities

54. Marriage should not be considered a bar to the appointment or to the continued employment of women teachers, nor should it affect remuneration or other conditions of work.

55. Employers should be prohibited from terminating contracts of service for reasons of pregnancy and maternity leave.

56. Arrangements such as crèches or nurseries should be considered where desirable to take care of the children of teachers with family responsibilities.

57. Measures should be taken to permit women teachers with family responsibilities to obtain teaching posts in the locality of their homes and to enable married couples, both of whom are teachers, to teach in the same general neighbourhood or in one and the same school.

58. In appropriate circumstances women teachers with family responsibilites who have left the profession before retirement age should be encouraged to return to teaching.

. . . .

IX. Conditions for Effective Teaching and Learning

. . . .

102. Effect should be given to the standards laid down by the International Labour Organisation in the field of maternity protection, and in particular the Maternity Protection Convention, 1919, and the Maternity Protection Convention (Revised), 1952, as well as to the standards referred to in Paragraph 126 of this Recommendation.

103. Women teachers with children should be encouraged to remain in the service by such measures as enabling them, at their request, to take additional unpaid leave of up to one year after childbirth without loss of employment, all rights resulting from employment being fully safeguarded.

. . . .

Notes

[1] Similar provisions are contained in the Nursing Personnel Recommendation, 1977 (No. 157).

[2] See Maternity Protection Recommendation, 1952 (No. 95).

LABOUR ADMINISTRATION 7

Texts adopted by the International Labour Conference

(1) Labour Inspection Convention, 1947 (No. 81)[1]

. . . .

Article 8

Both men and women shall be eligible for appointment to the inspection staff: where necessary, special duties may be assigned to men and women inspectors.

. . . .

(1) Labour Inspection (Agriculture) Convention, 1969 (No. 129)

. . . .

Article 6

1. The functions of the system of labour inspection in agriculture shall be–

(a) to secure the enforcement of the legal provisions relating to conditions of work and the protection of workers while engaged in their work, such as provisions relating to hours, wages, weekly rest and holidays, safety, health and welfare, the employment of women, children and young persons, and other connected matters, in so far as such provisions are enforceable by labour inspectors;

. . . .

Texts adopted by ILO Regional Conferences

Resolution concerning Labour Inspection, adopted by the Asian Regional Conference (Nuwara Eliya (Ceylon), 1950)

. . . .

6. (2) The inspection services should include an adequate number of women inspectors.

. . . .

Resolution concerning the Employment and Conditions of Work of Women in African Countries, adopted by the Second African Regional Conference (Addis Ababa, 1964)

. . . .

11. Appropriate numbers of women should be included in the initial and further training provided for labour inspectors (including factory inspectors), and women should be appointed to and advanced in labour inspection work according to their qualifications.

. . . .

Texts adopted by ILO Industrial Meetings, etc.

Conclusions (No. 2) concerning Conditions of Employment and Related Problems in the Leather Industry, with Particular Reference to Countries in the course of Industrialisation, adopted by the Tripartite Technical Meeting for the Leather and Footwear Industry (Geneva, 1969)

MEASURES FOR PRACTICAL APPLICATION

20. Because of the existing divergences between regulations and practice in many countries, measures should be taken, by the public authorities or by workers, employers and their organisations, to ensure the effective application of provisions concerning conditions of employment of workers in the industry, particularly in rural areas, small undertakings and handicraft workshops and in regard to women and young workers.

21. For this purpose, the improvement of inspection services in accordance with the provisions of the Labour Inspection Convention, 1947 (No. 81), should be regarded as a constant aim.

Note

[1] Principles for the organisation of inspection services had earlier been laid down in the Labour Inspection Recommendation, 1923 (No. 20), Paragraph 12 of which, in addition to providing that "the inspectorate should include women as well as men inspectors", stated that "while it is evident that with regard to certain matters and certain classes of work, inspection can be more suitably carried out by men, as in the case of other matters and other classes of work, inspection can be more suitably carried out by women, the women inspectors should in general have the same powers and duties and exercise the same authority as the men inspectors, subject to their having had the necessary training and experience, and should have equal opportunity of promotion to the higher ranks".